Brotherly Love

BROTHERLY LOVE

MURDER AND THE
POLITICS OF PREJUDICE
IN NINETEENTH-CENTURY
RHODE ISLAND

Charles and Tess Hoffmann

The University of Massachusetts Press
Amherst

Copyright © 1993 by
The University of Massachusetts Press
All rights reserved
Printed in the United States of America
LC 93-9959
ISBN 0-87023-852-3 (cloth); ISBN 1-55849-163-5 (pbk.)
Designed by Milenda Nan Ok Lee
Set in New Baskerville by Keystone Typesetting, Inc.
Printed and bound by Thomson-Shore, Inc.

Library of Congress Cataloging-in-Publication Data
Hoffmann, Charles.
Brotherly love : murder and the politics of prejudice in
nineteenth-century Rhode Island / Charles and Tess Hoffmann.
p. cm.
Includes bibliographical references and index.
ISBN 0-87023-852-3 (cloth: alk. paper).
ISBN 1-55849-163-5 (pbk.: alk. paper)
1. Murder—Rhode Island—History—19th century—Case studies.
2. Sprague, Amasa, 1798–1843. I. Hoffmann, Tess. II. Title.
HV6533.R4H64 1993
364.1'523'097451—dc20 93–9959
CIP
British Library Cataloguing in Publication data are available.

Except where noted, all illustrations are courtesy
of the Rhode Island Historical Society.

Contents

Illustrations

Acknowledgments

Our very special thanks to Diana Siegfried, interlibrary loan librarian at the Anacortes (Washington) library who tracked down for us various books, reports, and microfilm copies of the *Boston Pilot* from the Notre Dame University Library. It was her persistence and wide knowledge that made all the difference in the final stages of our research for this book.

The original research was completed while we still lived in Rhode Island. Our thanks go to the Rhode Island Historical Society, the John Hay Library (Brown University), the Providence College Library, Rhode Island College Library, and the Providence Public Library. Mark Brown at the John Hay, Linda Green and Tish Brennan at Rhode Island College, and Jean Richardson at the Providence Public were particularly helpful.

Also helpful was the Family History Center (Mt. Vernon, Washington) which provided us with copies of the 1840 and 1850 Cranston census.

Our personal thanks go to colleague Mark Estrin who proved invaluable in locating material and information still in Rhode Island which we needed for our research.

And finally, we greatly appreciate the work of Brett Lunsford of The Business (Anacortes) who made a special effort in copying some of the illustrations.

Preface

Beyond the personal tragedy that the 1843 murder of Yankee mill owner Amasa Sprague represented, its significance lies in the fact that three Irish brothers were arrested almost immediately for the crime. Two of the brothers, John and William Gordon, had immigrated to this country from Ireland only six months before; their older brother Nicholas had arrived six or seven years earlier. The Sprague family and the prosecution contended that Nicholas had sent for his brothers and incited them to murder Amasa Sprague because Sprague had made it impossible for Nicholas to get a tavern liquor license renewed by the Cranston (Rhode Island) Town Council. The Yankee residents of the small rural mill village where the murder took place, named Spraguesville after Amasa's father, sided with the Sprague family and searched for evidence that would point to the Gordons. Suspicious of foreigners in general and of Irish Catholic immigrants in particular, the villagers immediately focused on the Gordons as likely suspects, emphasizing the bitterness of the quarrel between Sprague and Gordon over the liquor license. The immediate arrest of the Gordon brothers on suspicion of murder even before any physical evidence against them had been found has suggested to contemporary and subsequent commentators that there was a prejudicial rush to judgment, resulting in a miscarriage of justice.

The social and political milieu in Rhode Island during the 1840s was complicated and fluid so that the circumstances surrounding the arrest and trials of the Gordon brothers were more complex than the ethnic and religious prejudice that underlay the attitudes of some Rhode Island Protestant Yankees against Irish Catholic immigrants. The murder and the trials took place in a period of change in Rhode Island when various and disparate forces were coming together to break down the semi-feudal

PREFACE

social order of the past. The old political order was based on a state
constitution that dated back more than a hundred years before the American Revolution. This constitution—actually, the Royal Charter founding
the colony in 1663—suited the Yankee farmers in sparsely populated
rural areas because it gave them more political power, and it was manipu-
lated by the Yankee industrialists, particularly the textile manufacturers
who established their mills in rural communities. Led by Thomas Wilson
Dorr, the movement to replace the old Royal Charter with a more egali-
tarian constitution was based on the American Revolutionary belief that
the powers and legitimacy of a state were derived from the people and the
people had the right to overturn an existing government to achieve its
will.

This movement for reform of the state constitution coincided with
events in Ireland that led to a vast increase in the number of Irish
immigrants to the United States in the 1840s, particularly in Massachusetts and Rhode Island, changing an old homogeneous Protestant Yankee
culture to a heterogenous one. In Rhode Island these immigrants, the
majority of them very poor, had no political power, for under the old
constitution suffrage was limited to native-born white males and, because
of an additional real property requirement, to a landowning class. The
reformers sought to enfranchise all adult white male immigrants who
became naturalized American citizens. Conservatives became alarmed at
the threat represented by the radical reformers joining forces with the
disenfranchised immigrants in their attempt to establish a rival democratic government. The conservatives defeated Dorr's rebellion by a show
of force and drove Dorr into exile.

The politics of prejudice in Rhode Island was a combination of political,
social, and economic factors that were exploited by conservatives, led by
Henry B. Anthony, editor of the *Providence Journal,* to oppose Dorr's
reforms. Playing on the religious and ethnic fears and prejudices of native
Americans against the Irish, Anthony raised the specter of Irish Catholics
taking over the state. Dorr, upon returning to Rhode Island on October 31, 1843, was immediately arrested for treason.

Two months later, on December 31, Amasa Sprague was brutally murdered. Sprague represented the old stable social and political order that
had been threatened by Dorr's reform movement. John, William, and
Nicholas Gordon were convenient suspects, and all the investigation was

directed toward proving them guilty. These three Irish brothers were victims of the broader social forces that underlie our narrative.

Our focus, however, is on the fundamental level of narrative—who did what, when, where—as the story of the murder of Amasa Sprague unfolds. The whole village of Spraguesville was involved in the case, and the villagers were witnesses at the three trials of the Gordon brothers. For example, Abner Sprague, Amasa's cousin, was the last man other than the murderer to see him alive. Michael Costello, an Irish servant in the Sprague household, stumbled upon the body as he made his way home from work. Dr. Israel Bowen, the local doctor and nearest physician, identified the corpse. Nathan Pratt, a boarder at a nearby boardinghouse serving the mill workers, found the murder weapon. David Lawton, a village resident, discovered the bloodied coat worn by one of the murderers. The investigation was a community effort directed by U.S. Senator William Sprague, the victim's brother. The mosaic of circumstantial evidence was pieced together by the prosecution from the testimony of scores of witnesses residing in the village, each contributing his or her bit to the pattern. William Sprague fitted the pieces together.

Nicholas Gordon had challenged Amasa Sprague's power and influence both politically and personally. The prosecution's theory was that the two younger brothers acting out of blind brotherly love killed Sprague to avenge their older brother's sense of wrong. This perverted brotherly love was contrasted by the prosecution with the idealized brotherly love of Amasa and William Sprague. Brotherly love was a motif played upon by both the prosecution and the defense counsels.

In the existing climate of anti-Irish, anti-Catholic prejudice the accusation of the Gordon brothers would obviously appease a natural sense of community outrage at the brutal murder of its wealthiest and most influential citizen. But if the Gordons were innocent, as many commentators have since concluded, then who was guilty? The solution to the 150-year-old mystery is forever locked in the secrets of a community that itself died in 1873 when the Sprague industrial empire went bankrupt. But it is possible to speculate on an alternative story of motive and conspiracy in the murder of Amasa Sprague. This alternate theory is offered in the spirit of conjecture rather than fact; after all this time, the truth remains a mystery.

Whoever actually murdered Amasa Sprague, it was John Gordon who

was found guilty and hanged, satisfying the state prosecution but not necessarily the public conscience. Gordon was the last man to be executed for
murder in Rhode Island. In 1852, partly because of a perceived miscarriage of justice in the Gordon case, Rhode Island abolished capital punishment. All the major arguments for capital punishment—deterrence,
retributive justice, preservation of the basic social order, and a hoped-for
moral redemption of the murderer—were evident in the state's trial and
speedy execution of John Gordon. All the main arguments against capital
punishment—the doubtful evidence of deterrence, the dubious ethics of
retribution by the state, the possibility of racial-ethnic discrimination, and
the danger of executing an innocent person—were equally evident in the
case. Whatever the pros and cons of all the other arguments for and
against capital punishment, what stands out in the Gordon case after all
these years is that a miscarriage of justice occurred because of ethnic and
religious prejudice against Irish immigrants in the 1840s. By the time
capital punishment was abolished in Rhode Island, it was too late for John
Gordon. He had been dead seven years, the current average in the United
States between conviction and execution for murder.

Guemes Island, Washington
February 1993

Chronology

June 27, 1842. The Rhode Island constitutional crisis known as the Dorr Rebellion ends in the defeat of the Dorrite troops. Thomas Dorr flees to exile in New Hampshire.

November 21–23, 1842. A new state constitution is ratified, effective May 1, 1843. Under its provisions naturalized citizens who owned property worth $134 and who had resided in the state for at least two years were qualified to vote.

June 1843. Ellen Gordon, her three sons (William, John, and Robert), her daughter, Margaret, and her granddaughter (William's daughter) arrive in Boston from Ireland. They join Nicholas in Spraguesville, a mill village in the town of Cranston.

July 24, 1843. Nicholas Gordon's liquor license is denied renewal by unanimous vote of the Cranston Town Council after Amasa Sprague, the mill owner, and others oppose it.

October 31, 1843. Ex-governor Dorr is arrested under an indictment for high treason against the state of Rhode Island.

December 31, 1843. Amasa Sprague is murdered.

January 1, 1844. Nicholas and John Gordon are arrested and charged with suspicion of murder. Their house is searched.

January 2, 1844. Ellen Gordon and her two sons William and Robert are also arrested. Ellen and Robert are later released.

January 12, 1844. John and William Gordon are bound over for grand jury investigation on murder charges.

January 15, 1844. Nicholas Gordon is bound over for grand jury investigation on an accessory before the fact murder charge.

January 17, 1844. William Sprague, Amasa's brother, resigns his seat in the U.S. Senate in order to take charge of the murder investigation and of the A. & W. Sprague Company, which runs the Cranston Print Works as well as other enterprises.

February 29, 1844. Dorr's treason trial is set for April 26 in Newport.

March 27, 1844. John and William Gordon are indicted for the murder of Amasa Sprague, Nicholas as an assessory before the fact. The trial is set for April 8.

April 17, 1844. John Gordon is found guilty of murder. William is acquitted. Nicholas is to be tried separately.

April 19, 1844. John Gordon's petition for a new trial and his sentencing is postponed by the court until October.

May 7, 1844. Dorr is found guilty of treason.

June 25, 1844. Dorr is sentenced to life imprisonment at hard labor in solitary confinement at the state prison in Providence.

June 27, 1844. Dorr is taken to the state prison where the two Gordon brothers are still imprisoned.

October 10, 1844. John Gordon's petition for a new trial and a postponement of sentence are denied by the state supreme court. He is sentenced to be hanged February 14, 1845.

October 22, 1844. Nicholas Gordon's first trial ends in a "hung jury" (eight for conviction, four for acquittal). He is bound over to be tried again.

November 2, 1844. Nicholas Gordon, although not convicted, is stricken from the list of qualified voters by the Cranston Town Council.

January 14, 1845. John Gordon's petition to the Rhode Island General Assembly for reprieve and suspension of sentence until after Nicholas's second trial is rejected by a vote of 36 to 27.

February 10, 1845. John Gordon petitions the governor for a stay of execution. His petition is accompanied by affidavits from William Gordon and Simon Mathewson (a juror in Nicholas Gordon's first trial). The petition is denied.

February 14, 1845. John Gordon is hanged in the yard of the state prison, Providence.

February 16, 1845. The large funeral procession for John Gordon moves through Spraguesville and the streets of Providence to the North Burial Ground.

April 17, 1845. The second Nicholas Gordon trial again ends with the jury unable to agree (three for conviction, nine for acquittal). Nicholas is released on bail provided by members of the Irish community and over the prosecution's objections.

June 27, 1845. Dorr is freed from prison by act of the state legislature, which is signed by the newly elected governor.

October 22, 1846. Nicholas Gordon dies in Providence, leaving debts totaling $1,322.65.

June 18, 1850. William Gordon is imprisoned for debt. Writ is also brought against Ellen Gordon.

February 1852. The Rhode Island legislature votes to abolish capital punishment, substituting life imprisonment and loss of all civil rights. The death penalty remains in force for murder committed by anyone serving a life sentence.

December 27, 1854. Thomas Wilson Dorr dies at age forty-nine.

October 19, 1856. William Sprague dies of typhoid fever, in the midst of building his largest mill at Baltic, Connecticut.

October 1873. The Sprague industrial empire collapses in bankruptcy, the largest business failure in the nation's history at the time.

Brotherly Love

CHAPTER ONE

The Murder

On a very cold New Year's Eve in 1843, Michael Costello, who was employed as a servant in the mansion house of wealthy textile manufacturer Amasa Sprague, left work about sundown, probably no later than 4:15 P.M., to return to his boardinghouse on the old Plainfield Turnpike, about a mile away. Since the mansion house was on the Cranston Road, he would have taken it rather than the private road that ran north to the Sprague mill complex with its calico cloth printing works, company store, and numerous duplexes and boardinghouses for the factory workers, all owned by Amasa Sprague and his brother William. A few hundred yards west was Nicholas Gordon's house which had an addition that contained a store and, until recently, a tavern patronized by the workers. Turning right before reaching the Gordon house, Costello walked north on the road to the schoolhouse where he turned left, following the cartway (also known as the driftway) across a swampy area called Hawkins' Hole and up the hill to the footbridge over Pochasset Brook which formed the border between the Rhode Island towns of Cranston and Johnston.

It probably took him about fifteen minutes to reach the footbridge over the brook. There were several inches of snow on the ground, and the packed snow on the wooden bridge was slippery. His dinner pail in his left hand, Costello grasped the railing with his right hand and moved carefully. In the middle of the bridge he saw blood on the snow. He followed the trail of blood to the far end of the bridge; five or six yards beyond he saw the body of a man spread-eagled face down on the snow. Costello stopped and stared at the body. There was no one about. Sensing he could do nothing for the man who lay there, he ran to the nearest house on the Plainfield Road and raised the alarm.[1]

A group of men accompanied him back to where the body lay. By now,

1

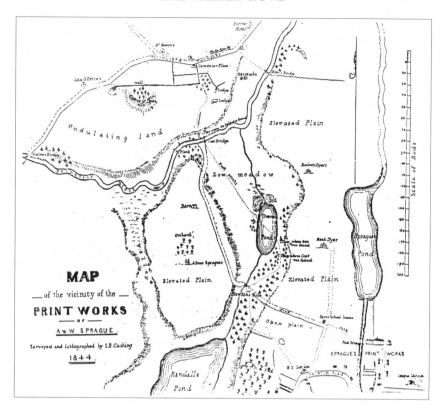

Map of the vicinity of the print works of A. & W. Sprague, 1844. S. B. Cushing, surveyor.

although there was still light in the sky, the sun had set. On close examination they saw that the man had been beaten to death, but the head had been so disfigured that the murdered man's face was unrecognizable. In the fading light, young Thornton, a neighbor's son, thought the victim was his father. But someone else said it was Amasa Sprague because the frock coat resembled the one he habitually wore. By then, Dr. Israel Bowen had arrived from the town of Johnston with another group of neighbors. They turned the body over, face up, and the dead man was identified by Dr. Bowen as Amasa Sprague.

Sunday afternoon, December 31, 1843, had begun normally for Sprague as he sat down to a hearty dinner with his wife, Fanny, and their four children, Mary Anna, Almira, Amasa, and William. The only worry on his mind at the moment was the welfare of the stock free-grazing at his farm which was about a mile from the house. There was no barn there in which to shelter them. With at least six inches of old snow on the ground and the promise of a clear, cold night, he had decided to visit the farm and check on the stock himself rather than depend on the young tenant farmer who lived on the place. This did not surprise his wife, since he often walked there in the afternoon after dinner, even on Sundays, a fact well known in the village.

The increasing cold must have been very much on his mind, because when he set out for the farm shortly after three o'clock, he stopped first at the print works furnace room to talk to Edward Coil, who was in charge of the fires. Sprague wanted to be sure there was enough heat maintained in the boilers for the steam engine to run the complicated printing machines on Monday morning, given that they were idle on Sunday.[2]

Sprague left the furnace room about 3:30 P.M., having talked with Coil for only a short while. He took the private path just west of the print works, the more direct route. The driftway was often used during the week by the villagers as a shortcut to the Plainfield Turnpike, and it was used on Sundays by local hunters poaching small game. Amasa was next seen by his cousin, Abner Sprague, around 3:30 P.M. on the path halfway between Hawkins' Hole and Abner's farmhouse, about 100 yards north of the swamp. Abner was the last man to see Amasa alive, other than the murderer or murderers, for Amasa never reached his farm.

To the men gathered around Sprague's body, the timing of the murder and the severity of the blows seemed to suggest an angry confrontation and a vicious assault rather than a coldly planned, premeditated murder. Whatever the motivation, there was no doubt in Dr. Bowen's mind that Sprague had been murdered. He had been struck on the left side of the head with a blunt instrument with enough force to fracture the skull and rupture the brain membrane. Another heavy blow on the right side of the head, also fracturing the skull, could equally well have caused death. Amasa was a large and powerful man, athletic in appearance and physically fit. He could not have been attacked without a struggle, and there was evidence in the trampled snow around the body that he had defended himself against the attack. But a gunshot wound on his right forearm near the wrist, which had broken the small bone of the arm, suggested that he had first been disabled and then beaten to death.

Darkness was setting in, and the search for evidence was about to be postponed until the morning when one of the villagers, Stephen Mathewson, found a pistol under the bridge on the Johnston side, only a few yards from the body. The pistol was turned over to Robert Wilson, coroner for the town of Johnston. Its percussion lock had been snapped in an attempt to fire it, but the gun had failed to fire and evidently had been thrown under the bridge.

The coroner had been contacted immediately by Dr. Bowen so that he could hold an inquest on the spot. Wilson, only thirty-four years old, had a heavy responsibility placed on him, for this was no ordinary death; a prominent citizen had been brutally murdered. By six o'clock Wilson had contacted the town sergeant who rounded up a jury, and the coroner empanelled them at the scene of the murder. The only light came from a small lantern that cast an eerie glow on the scene, highlighting the wounds but throwing everything else into shadow and darkness. The body was examined briefly by the jury, enough to determine the cause of death. Only then was the body of Amasa Sprague released to his friends and neighbors. A teamster carried it home in his wagon.

Robert Wilson and the jury adjourned to Dr. Bowen's house on the Plainfield Road, across from the Carpenter place that had been Amasa's destination. One of the jurors, Albert Waterman, examined the pistol and, taking his pen-knife, drew the wad of paper from the charge. The gunpowder and ball were put into a phial to be handed later to the examining officer at the state prison. The wad of paper was a piece of the *Boston Pilot,* an Irish Catholic newspaper. In the absence of any clues or evidence pointing to any particular person, the jury could only conclude that Amasa Sprague had been murdered by a person or persons unknown. No motive for the murder could be ascertained; the fact that a valuable gold watch and sixty dollars in cash were left untouched on the body ruled out robbery. The coroner concluded that some unknown person had come up behind Sprague and knocked him off the bridge with a heavy blow to the head. The murderer probably had an accomplice, as the pistol and the struggle in the snow suggested.

The body of Amasa Sprague was taken to his house and placed on the floor in one of the front parlors. The head and shoulders were slightly elevated to give the body a more peaceful appearance, but there was no hiding the fact that Sprague had been brutally beaten about the head and face. The position of the gunshot wound suggested that Amasa raised his right arm to protect his head from further blows when the bullet struck his arm. Dr. Bowen had been called in originally because he was the nearest physician, living only a quarter of a mile from the scene of the murder. It was not until half past nine that Dr. Lewis L. Miller, the family physician, examined the body to declare what everyone already knew: that the cause of death was the blow to the head by a blunt instrument, probably the edge of a musket guard. The breech of a gun could have caused the fatal blows to the skull on the left temple. Since Dr. Miller examined the body several hours after it was brought home, he could not estimate the time of death.

A steady stream of friends and neighbors hearing of the murder came to the house to pay their last respects, to console the widow and children, and then to gather in small groups on the road outside to speculate on who the murderer or murderers might be. There was no doubt in their minds that somebody in Spraguesville was guilty. The Kingstons, who lived less than a half-mile from the Sprague mansion on the Cranston road to Providence, were typical of the neighbors who went to the Sprague house that night. John and William Kingston, like most of the villagers, worked in the print works, and one of their sisters and their brother Thompson were in service at the Sprague house and actually lived there. They had been celebrating New Year's Eve at King's Tavern, a half-mile from their house on the way to Providence. Between four and five o'clock John Gordon, a fellow Irishman, had joined the Kingstons at their house and went with them to the tavern. Sometime between six and seven o'clock the Kingston brothers and John Gordon had gone back to the Kingstons' house, and shortly after that the Kingstons' sister arrived to tell them all of the murder. Their brother Thompson, who had spent the day in Providence, returned home to learn the news of the murder and to accompany his mother, sister, and brothers to view the body. Their friend John Gordon went with them as far as the gate of the Sprague house but did not enter, continuing instead toward his brother Nicholas's house a few hundred yards down the road toward the print works.

There were many rumors circulating that night about the murderer.[3] One had it that Amasa had been on his way to see his mistress and had been waylaid by an irate husband, but no names were suggested and the rumor died for want of specifics. Another was that one of the employees at the print works, a laborer known simply as Big Peter, held a grudge against Amasa Sprague; but this rumor also died for want of details.

One speculation that would certainly have been in the air was that Sprague may have been the victim of political assassination. Political tensions were still very high in Rhode Island in the aftermath of the recent insurrection known as the Dorr Rebellion. Thomas Wilson Dorr, the leader of a reform movement that would have given the vote to all adult white male citizens, had set up a rival state government and army and attempted to seize the state arsenal. Defeated, Dorr had been arrested for treason on October 31, 1843, exactly two months before Amasa Sprague's murder. Since Amasa Sprague, his brother William, and their brother-in-law Emanuel Rice had been instrumental in bringing about Dorr's downfall, the possibility of a political assassination would be very much on the minds of the villagers. This was a plausible motive for the murder, but there was no obvious suspect at whom to point an accusing finger. Dorr was in solitary confinement in the state prison, his supporters in total disarray.

But there was one rumor that persisted and survived, for it had a suspect to focus on and plenty of details to give it flesh. It was that Nicholas Gordon, older brother of John and William, held a grudge against Amasa Sprague over the loss of his liquor license the previous summer. Amasa had openly opposed the license's renewal on the grounds that his workers were neglecting their duties and getting drunk during working hours at Nicholas Gordon's store.

One villager, Richard Knight, had reason to remember the quarrel, for he had attended all the town council meetings that discussed Gordon's application for renewal of his liquor license. Knight ran a boardinghouse near Sprague's house, taking in workers from the print works. He and Charles Searle, Amasa's agent, had objected to the renewal on orders from Sprague and had presented a remonstrance signed by them and other villagers, as well as by some of the Irish workers at the mill. Knight had observed the open hostility between Gordon and Sprague at a town council meeting, and he had personally warned Amasa that Gordon was out to get him, but Amasa had laughed at him.[4]

Stories about the hostility between Sprague and Gordon proliferated. For example, someone in the village reported that one day Amasa and Nicholas had met on the village pathway; neither would step aside until Amasa grabbed Nicholas by the collar and threw him to one side, shouting, "Get out of the way, you damned Irishman."[5] Another villager, Hardin Hudson, remembered that Nicholas had threatened Amasa, say-

Amasa Sprague (1798–1843), about 1839

ing that he would have his revenge and "come up with him." Somebody else conjectured that Nicholas had brought his brothers over in order to get revenge. Irish families were known to stick together: one brother's enemy would be the enemy of all the others. Patrick Conley and Matthew Smith suggest in *Catholicism in Rhode Island* that "it appeared to many [in Rhode Island] that this heinous crime was an instance of the infamous

'Whiteboy' outrages that Irish peasants had visited upon their opponents throughout the early nineteenth century."[6] A "Whiteboy" was a member of an illegal association of Irish peasants formed in 1760 to resist their landlords' collection of taxes and tithes. From such a premise it was only a short step to conjecture that William and John Gordon would do whatever their older brother told them to do, even kill, for why else would Nicholas send for them to come all the way from Ireland. The fact that Nicholas had sent for them before the quarrel with Amasa Sprague broke out was no deterrence to the rumor. Indeed, the rumors grew even more inventive. One had it that Amasa Sprague was murdered because he had taken one of the Gordon wives as his mistress, until somebody pointed out that none of the Gordon brothers was married, and William was a widower. It was obviously much easier for the Yankee villagers to think one of the Irish had committed the murder than to suspect one of their own had planned it—a Sprague, for example.

The day after the murder a special town meeting in Cranston (at which propertyless Irish immigrants had no voice or vote) was called to order at which Sheldon Knight, a member of the town council, was appointed chair. The meeting authorized the town council to offer a reward of one thousand dollars for information leading to the conviction of the murderer. The meeting further resolved that it was the duty of the community as a whole "to ferret out the perpetrator or perpetrators of this atrocious murder, that he or they may be brought to justice." Toward that end vigilance committees were appointed in the several school districts as well as a central committee to receive and correlate all the information that the vigilance committees and citizens received. Informants were spurred by an additional reward of one thousand dollars offered by the Sprague family for information leading to the conviction of the murderer or murderers.[7]

In this atmosphere of suspicion, the rumors and stories about Nicholas Gordon's threats against Amasa Sprague were brought to the attention of the central committee from various sources. By 6:00 P.M. or thereabouts on Monday, January 1, 1844, Nicholas and John Gordon had been arrested on suspicion of murder, even though not one piece of physical evidence linking the Gordons to the crime had yet been discovered.

That same day Nicholas and John Gordon were brought before the justice of the peace in Providence, Henry L. Bowen, a prominent city lawyer, who committed them to prison for examination at a later date.

The *Providence Journal* reported the next day that the grounds for suspicion, besides Nicholas Gordon's threats against Amasa Sprague, were that Nicholas "has been seen repeatedly, within the last week, with a gun in his hand, near where Mr. S. [Sprague] was found," a false rumor. The *Providence Journal* correctly reported that "his premises have been searched, and no gun can be found on them, although it is well known that he had one." Nicholas Gordon was identified as a freeman of the town of Cranston and as an Irishman.[8]

The next day almost all the remaining members of the Gordon family were arrested, including the mother, Ellen Gordon, and her youngest son, Robert. Both were discharged later that same day, the mother after making contradictory statements and the son Robert after being able to prove he was not in Cranston the day of the murder. William Gordon, also arrested, was committed to prison for later examination on suspicion of murder, as was Michael O'Brien, a friend of Nicholas Gordon, because he "was seen in company with the Gordons on Sunday [the day of the murder], and was known to have had a difficulty with Mr. Sprague."[9]

Also arrested that same day was Nicholas Gordon's dog, on the grounds that alongside the tracks of Amasa leading to the swamp were those of a dog. The dog was described by the *Providence Journal* as ferocious, wearing "a collar of jagged metal, and some of the wounds upon Mr. Sprague are such as would be made by such a collar on a dog springing at his throat." Gordon's dog was later described by a defense attorney as being "too feeble and harmless to hurt a living being—who can but just walk, and who has not a tooth left in his head."[10]

The following day, Wednesday, the *Providence Journal* described the evidence that was to play such a prominent part in the case against the Gordons: tracks in the snow near the body had been followed to a nearby swamp, where "a coat marked with blood was found in it, and a gun, much battered and broken in two. The gun has been identified as belonging to [Nicholas] Gordon." The coat had a hole in the elbow, "and a shirt found in Gordon's house has a bloody stain on the sleeve corresponding to the hole in the coat." In addition, "two men were seen going toward the fatal spot shortly before the murder. Two men were seen to emerge from the swamp on the other side after the deed had been committed; one of them without his coat." Wet boots, spots of what looked like blood on clothes and bedsheets, and wet clothes found under a bed in the Gordon house rounded out the evidence. The reporter assumed that Nicholas Gordon with his brother John were the two men seen in the vicinity of the murder and concluded that they were "the guilty parties."[11]

The legal distinction between authorized sheriff's officers and ordinary villagers had been totally ignored in the search for clues and the gathering of information. The Sprague family itself, led by Senator William Sprague, had directed the gathering of evidence against the Gordons. The Gordon house had been searched, the store broken into, and the scene of the crime trampled in the search for clues that would implicate the Gordons.

On Friday, January 5, Amasa Sprague's funeral took place at his home, attended by "a very large concourse of people, neighbors and friends, and citizens from other towns, assembled to manifest their respect for the deceased, and their sympathy with the family and relatives."[12] Understandably, no member of the Gordon family attended the funeral, but the fact that none of the Gordon brothers had visited the Sprague house to pay his respects was cited in the *Journal* as implied evidence of guilt.[13]

In the same column in which it reported the details of Amasa Sprague's funeral, the *Journal* branded as a slanderous lie a letter from a Providence citizen published in the *New York Herald* questioning the guilt of John and Nicholas Gordon. To reinforce its claim that the two Gordon brothers were guilty, the *Journal* cited the alleged testimony of "a girl, ten years of age, who lived in the family of Nicholas Gordon" and whose statement fastened "suspicion more strongly upon those arrested." Since the only child living in the Gordon household at the time was the seven-year-old daughter of William Gordon, and since no other reference was ever made to her testimony, if any, before or during the trial, the *Journal* seems to have been misinformed. The newspaper also treated as rumor a claim that Nicholas Gordon had *not* threatened Amasa Sprague. To give the paper credit, it did publish a correction of the report in the previous week's issue of the *Chronicle* that Michael O'Brien, who had been arrested along with Nicholas Gordon, had been charged with the rape of a little girl and had received a short sentence: it was another Michael O'Brien, and he had been convicted of assault with intent to commit rape and had been sentenced to four years, "and is now serving out his sentence."[14]

On Friday, January 12, the three Gordon brothers were brought before Henry L. Bowen, the justice of the peace, who had jailed them on suspicion of murder. It was the first time since January 1 that the three brothers had been in the same room together. William had tried to visit his brothers in prison on January 2, but was denied access to them. He himself had been arrested by a sheriff's posse on his way home that day and imprisoned in a separate cell. He had attempted to talk to Nicholas in the office of the justice of the peace but had been restrained from doing so by the officers.

The examination of the Gordon brothers and Michael O'Brien was held in secret. Former Attorney General Albert C. Greene appeared for the State, and Samuel Currey and John P. Knowles for the prisoners. John and William Gordon were committed for possible trial during the March term of the supreme court, following a grand jury investigation. The supreme court heard all cases involving capital offenses. The examination of O'Brien and Nicholas Gordon was adjourned until Monday, at which time Nicholas was also bound over to the grand jury for indictment; Michael O'Brien was discharged. The following day William Sprague resigned his Senate seat to devote himself to the coming trial and its prosecution.

Nicholas Gordon had much to worry him as he sat in solitary confinement in the state prison during the two months between his arrest on suspicion of murder and his indictment as an accessory to murder. He had an alibi for the time of the murder, having been in Providence all that Sunday afternoon until after the time Sprague's body was discovered. Yet in spite of that he had been arrested on suspicion of murder and his alibi was seen as a deliberate arrangement to be elsewhere while others murdered Sprague.

The case against the Gordons appeared strong—the bloodied coat found hidden near the murder site and the gun used as the murder weapon were both linked to Nicholas and his brothers. Furthermore, he had publicly quarreled with Amasa Sprague; there was no denying it, and although he had not done the murder himself, the quarrel was seen as a motive for getting others to do it, namely his brothers John and William.

What was foremost in his mind was the question of what had happened to the gun he kept in the store. If it could be produced, the case against him and his brothers would be severely weakened. He believed the gun must have been knocked down by the dog and fallen behind a barrel. That would explain why the gun had not been found. Right from the beginning he begged Dr. Cleaveland, the jailer, to go to Cranston to search for it, but Cleaveland could not find it anywhere in the store, nor could anybody else. The gun was inexplicably missing.

In the same state prison, also in solitary confinement awaiting trial, was Thomas Dorr, charged with treason. The great difference between them (aside from the fact that treason was a noncapital offense) was that, for all his political enemies, Dorr was a member of the governing elite, and had friends in high places, including a future governor of the state, his uncle Philip Allen. Although he would be convicted for his crime, he would eventually be pardoned when his friends came to power. In contrast, Nicholas Gordon was an ordinary man with little if any political influence. Although he had been declared a freeman of the town in 1842, he was also, as an Irishman, a member of a group that was largely disenfranchised, politically powerless, and generally the object of religious and political prejudice and hostility.

CHAPTER TWO

Background to Murder

The history of Rhode Island's constitutional crisis known as the Dorr Rebellion provides an essential background to an understanding of the politics of prejudice that operated during the trials of the Gordon brothers for the murder of Amasa Sprague. Directly and indirectly, the quarrel between Nicholas Gordon and Amasa Sprague over the renewal of Gordon's liquor license was related to the social and political tensions in the state during and after the Dorr Rebellion. While these tensions were largely indirect and implicit in the first trial, that of John and William Gordon, they were direct and explicit in the two separate trials of Nicholas Gordon. The recent arrest and the impending trial for treason of Thomas Wilson Dorr had brought the political conflict between reformers and conservatives into the foreground in the public mind and revived the fears of physical violence generated by the Dorr Rebellion a year and a half earlier.

Thomas Wilson Dorr was a Protestant of Irish descent whose grandfather had left Ireland in time to take part in the American Revolution and ride with Paul Revere on his famous excursion. Sullivan Dorr, his father, was a self-made man who was successful in shipping and commerce after the Revolution; he had allied himself with one of the leading Rhode Island families, the Allens, by marrying the daughter of Zachariah Allen, Sr. After an elite education at Phillips Exeter Academy and Harvard College, Thomas Dorr went into politics, allying himself with the urban, more liberal wing of the Democratic Party at odds with the agrarian conservative Democrats like the Spragues over the issue of constitutional reforms and suffrage.[1]

Until 1842, Rhode Island functioned under the original Royal Charter of 1663, which was liberal in its seventeenth-century context by emphasiz-

ing religious freedom, but by nineteenth-century standards was reaction-
ary in its restrictive suffrage qualifications and legislative apportionment
provisions. Under the Royal Charter, the right to vote was limited to
native-born white males who owned real estate and had lived in the state
more than two years.[2] In effect this meant that by the 1830s only about
one-third of the adult white male population was eligible to vote. Furthermore, since each township, no matter how rural and sparsely populated,
was entitled to at least one representative in the general assembly, the
large industrial centers with their increasing number of foreign-born,
disenfranchised residents were proportionately underrepresented. Reforms such as the elimination of restrictive electoral laws, a more independent judiciary, and reform of the penal code were practical and seemingly
mild liberalizations even by mid-nineteenth-century political standards.
Neighboring Massachusetts, for example, as well as many other states of
the Northeast and West had liberalized voting qualifications over twenty
years before, generally extending the franchise to all male adults who
paid any kind of tax.[3]

The one truly radical aspect of Dorr's movement was the attempt to
apply the ideological principles of the American Revolution to nineteenth-century Rhode Island. The Dorrites not only sought to include the
Bill of Rights in the state constitution, which other states had done over a
half century earlier, but they also insisted that "all political power and
sovereignty are originally vested in, and of right belonging to the people
. . . [who have the right] to alter, reform, or totally change [the govern-
ment] whenever their safety or happiness requires."[4] This paraphrase of
the Declaration of Independence was at the center of the rationale for
Dorr's Rebellion and constituted the political philosophy by which the
adoption of a new constitution, the People's Constitution, was justified. In
December 1841, the People's Constitution was overwhelmingly ratified by
nearly 14,000 electors who met the qualifications—white male citizens of
the United States of the age of twenty-one or more years who had resided
in the state one year.[5]

Conservatives of both political parties (the urban Whigs and the rural
Democrats) reacted quickly to the threat, challenging the philosophical
and legal basis of Dorr's movement. An *ex cathedra* opinion by the three
justices of the Rhode Island supreme court (Durfee, Haile, and Staples)
was published in March 1842, declaring the People's Constitution illegal
and having no "binding force," and asserting that any attempt to put it

into effect would be treasonable.[6] In the same month, the conservative Landholders' Constitution narrowly failed of ratification, thereby encouraging the Dorrites to establish a rival government the following month based on their constitution with Dorr as governor.

On May 18, Dorr and his supporters decided to capture the state arsenal in Providence, an action precipitated by the fact that the state government under Governor King had garrisoned it with armed citizens. The assault on the arsenal was part symbolic gesture to assert Dorr's authority as governor, part practical tactics to gain weapons, and part *opéra bouffe*. Training two Revolutionary War cannons on the arsenal, the Dorrites demanded the garrison's surrender, a demand refused by Dorr's brother-in-law, Samuel Ames, who was in command. Despite the fact that his father, younger brother, and his uncle Zachariah Allen were all in the building, Dorr ordered the cannons to be fired. But the night was damp and foggy, and so was the gunpowder; both cannons failed to fire. The Dorrites retreated in ignominious defeat, and Dorr fled the state, aided by his uncle Crawford Allen.[7]

Dorr returned to the state on June 25 for one last attempt to rally his forces at Chepachet. This time the state government was ready for him with an overwhelming force of over 3,000 troops, a declaration of martial law, and the promise of aid from the militia of Connecticut and Massachusetts and even federal troops, if necessary. Realizing the hopelessness of the situation, Dorr dismissed his army of 500 men and again fled the state before the state militia arrived. Not a shot was fired, but the political repercussions echoed around the state.[8]

On the one hand, the new political majority in Rhode Island—a coalition of conservative Whigs and Democrats, calling themselves the Law and Order Party—persecuted suspected Dorrites under a set of repressive measures called the Algerine Law passed in April 1842. It was under this law that Dorr was indicted for treason in August 1842. On the other hand, a new constitutional convention was called by the state government, and at the urging of U.S. Senator William Sprague some concessions were made to electoral reform in the new constitution ratified in November 1842. Some provisions of the Bill of Rights, a more reasonable apportionment of seats in the House of Representatives, and a more independent judiciary were all included in the constitution. But the real estate property qualification for voting was retained, and of course the Dorrites had failed completely in their radical concept of popular sovereignty. On one important point the new constitution was more liberal than Dorr's constitution; it abolished slavery and reenfranchised the blacks by the simple expedient of deleting the word "white" from the phrase defining male, adult electors, a liberalization the Dorrites specifically rejected even though Dorr himself had urged giving the blacks the vote.[9]

Despite these liberalizing concessions, which they supported, the Spragues knew their political power depended on maintaining the old order. Generally, their Irish workers remained unenfranchised because of the property qualification. Those of their workers who could vote were carefully supervised in their voting by the Spragues and their agents. The new constitution made no provision for a secret ballot so that the corrupt practice of checking on the marking of ballots remained a common practice. As Peter J. Coleman suggests in *The Transformation of Rhode Island, 1790–1860,* it was "a method nicely calculated to secure the election of Sprague candidates, or, indeed, of the Spragues themselves." Furthermore, the real estate qualification itself fostered the corrupt practice of land changing hands on election day, "merely to enfranchise additional voters," or to the selling of "small parcels of realty by promissory note in a sum considerably in excess of the property's worth"; in the event that "the purchaser failed to vote according to instructions," the seller presented the note for payment.[10]

By these methods the Spragues maintained their political power as they had earlier under the Royal Charter. Nothing much changed politically under the new constitution, and the conservative Law and Order Party won the election mandated by the new constitution. Although conservative Democrats like Philip Allen and William Sprague "cultivated Irish support," Coleman concludes that "they regarded their workers as so many sheep to be herded to the polls, and they showed little interest in social or economic reform. Indeed, they behaved like feudal seigneurs, courting their employees' political support as one of the allegiances sealed in the labor contract."[11]

The Sprague brothers were descended from an old Rhode Island family. They could trace their paternal ancestry back six generations to William Sprague, son of Edward from Upway, England, who first settled in Salem, Massachusetts, in 1628. Their mother, Annie Potter, a farmer's daughter, was a direct descendant of Roger Williams, founder of the Rhode Island colony. Amasa Sprague, born in April 1798, was the oldest of the three sons of William and Annie. William was born the following year in November. Benoni, born in 1803, the youngest of the sons and baby of the family was the only child who did not enter the family business. He refused to have anything to do with the Sprague enterprise, and when his father died in 1836 he was given a legacy but no share in the Sprague Company. Even the daughters, Susanna, the oldest of the children, born in 1796, and Almira, played their role in the family business. Susanna and later Almira reeled the yarn that Amasa and William carded and spun at the cotton spinning mill. When the wooden mill was burnt to the ground in 1813 by an arsonist, a drastic and at the time a common form of labor protest, William Sprague built a stone mill on the site. Susanna married her father's clerk and general bookkeeper, Obadiah Mathewson, and moved with him to Baltimore, where William and other Providence merchants established a commission house to sell their cotton goods. Almira married Emanuel Rice who did so well superintending the cotton mills that he was left in charge whenever young William was away.[12]

The father, like Amasa later on, worked alongside his men in the print works when it was built in 1824. Like his son, he was a stout, strongly built man who looked more like a farmer than a businessman. Many of the workers, mostly of Yankee stock from the surrounding farms rather than immigrants, boarded at his house and both Amasa and William grew up surrounded by the talk of the mill. As soon as Amasa was old enough, he was sent to Groton, Connecticut, to open a store and to farm-out cotton yarn to be woven by the families in the adjoining villages. It was there, in the village of Poquonnoc, that Amasa met and married Fanny Morgan, daughter of the local shoemaker who was related to the John Pierpont Morgan family. In 1828, when his mother died, Amasa and his new family returned to Spraguesville, Amasa to help his father in the expanding business, Fanny to run the household for her father-in-law and bring up, in addition to her own children, those of her sister-in-law Susanna, who had died in 1824. After the death of his father in 1836, Amasa and the family continued to live in the mansion house while he ran the print works.[13]

At the center of the A. & W. (Amasa and William) Sprague Company was Spraguesville, a village of over five hundred people almost entirely dependent on the Spragues, who owned the "tenements" as well as the company store, for employment, housing, and provisions. The tenements were "tied cottages" rented by families who worked at the print works; the rent was deducted from their pay and if they stopped working at the mill, they had to vacate the tenement. Single men and casual laborers boarded at Richard Knight's or even at the Sprague house.

The mansion, that symbol of manorial paternalism in Rhode Island mill villages, was located within sight of the print works, as such mansions generally were. It had been built by William, the father, in the 1790s and enlarged in the early 1800s with the birth of the children. Both Amasa and William were born there, and Amasa lived in the house until the day he died, his body brought back home "to rest." Whatever the larger implications of Amasa Sprague's murder, the focus was Spraguesville, a nineteenth-century New England mill village owned by the company. Part of Amasa's power and influence was based on a traditional hierarchical social order—the paternalistic mill owner of old Yankee stock living in his mansion house surrounded by his "family" of workers living in boardinghouses or tied cottages near the mill, or even boarding at the mansion house itself. As Paul Goodman suggests in *Towards a Christian Republic*, the Spragues may have "pictured themselves as popular tribunes" as they sat down to meals with their employees "around an immense table at which Sprague [the father] presided";[14] but like any other paternalistic mill system in Rhode Island there never was any doubt as to who was tribune and who plebian.

Although the Spragues as textile manufacturers were the natural political allies of the conservative urban Democrats like the Allens, they were, according to Goodman, "wealthy outsiders, dissidents who possessed great resources and marketed themselves as champions of the masses, sturdy country men who resisted integration into the elite centered in Providence."[15] Socially and culturally they were miles apart from the Providence elite with their Brown University education, their European grand tours, their cultivated social manners, and their inherited fortunes acquired in the slave trade and the China opium trade and invested by them in textile manufacturing.

No matter how rural the setting of Spraguesville—after all, Amasa Sprague was on his way to the farm to check his herd of cattle when he was murdered—the Sprague Print Works was different from the usual mill village in that it was part of a profitable manufacturing business which included several Sprague-owned cotton mills in other villages. Indeed, the Sprague enterprise was an important part of the ever-expanding

The Sprague Mansion at 1351 Cranston Street, Spraguesville

textile manufacturing industry in Rhode Island and other southern New England states during the nineteenth century. Although agriculture was still the main occupation of these states in the 1830s, the farms were small, producing mainly for families and local markets. Textile manufacturing was the main form of industry in New England, and indeed the industrial revolution in America began with the establishment of the Slater cotton mill in Pawtucket, Rhode Island, in 1793. By 1832, there were 116 cotton mills in Rhode Island, employing 8,500 workers.[16] The Sprague cotton mills accounted for about 6 percent of all the operating looms in Rhode Island.[17] In the 1835–36 fiscal year about 120 million yards of calico cloth had been printed in the United States, mainly in Rhode Island and nearby Massachusetts.[18]

There were only two rival calico printing companies in the state large enough to compete with the Spragues. One was founded in 1830 by Philip Allen. By 1836, the Allen Print Works in Providence was turning out 130,000 yards of calico cloth a week on five printing machines and employing 250 workers.[19] The other competing company was owned by Benjamin Cozzens who reported a profit of $100,000 in the 1840 fiscal year. The Cranston Print Works would have been making at least as much profit, for by 1850 the Spragues were employing 200 workers and producing goods valued at $840,000.[20] And this was before the large expansion of the Sprague Company took effect under William Sprague.

Spraguesville, however, appeared no different from other rural Rhode Island villages of the time with its outlying farms, the cluster of factory buildings alongside the river, waterfall, and mill pond, the owner's mansion, and workers' cottages, the boardinghouses, the company store, and the Protestant church (built in 1825 on land donated by the Spragues), all within walking distance of each other, all within view of Amasa Sprague. The textile factory city developed by the Boston Manufacturing Company in Lowell, Massachusetts, in the 1820s was as different from the Rhode Island pattern as nineteenth-century city planning was from the eighteenth-century village ideal incorporated into the rural Rhode Island factory town.[21]

Whether the Rhode Island mill village was entirely planned from scratch, as was Zachariah Allen's Allendale in 1822, or imposed upon an existing agricultural community, as was Spraguesville, the village itself was a cohesive community dominated economically and socially by the mill owner. In one way, however, Sprague's workers differed: because the factory operated as a print works, printing patterns from engravings on cotton cloth manufactured elsewhere by cotton mills owned by the Spragues, more skilled male workers were needed to run the complex and expensive printing machinery than was the case in a cotton mill. Some of the operations, such as bleaching and dyeing, required only unskilled laborers, such as John Gordon, or women and children. But whereas women and children constituted about seven-eighths of the work force in cotton mills in 1832, they constituted only about one-third of the employees in calico print works.[22] Fewer employed women and children at the Cranston Print Works meant that Spraguesville tended to be made up of more single males in boardinghouses than families living in tenements.

Although the Sprague Company employed fewer women and children at the print works, it shared in the common practice of using child labor because the various cotton mills owned by the Spragues were an integral part of the calico printing enterprise. The family system was in contrast to the Lowell system of factory girls and women; "factory children were particularly numerous in Rhode Island."[23] Indeed, in 1831, Rhode Island cotton mills employed nearly 3,500 children under twelve years of age, "or three quarters of all the children reported working in American cotton mills."[24] As more and more immigrants arrived, Irish children replaced the indigenous work force in the factories. In 1833, a labor organizer for the New England Workingmen's Association based in Fall

River, Massachusetts, complained of forty children between the ages of six and ten working full time in one of the screw factories in Providence.[25] In the 1850s, two such factories in Providence employed 225 children under the age of fifteen, half of whom worked the night shift. By that time, the situation had improved in the textile mills, but only because technological advances had made the hiring of children under the age of twelve unnecessary.[26]

Wages were correspondingly low for children and women. A skilled adult male mechanic could earn as much as $9.00 a week and the average adult male mill worker earned $4.50 a week in 1832, but when the women and children, the bulk of the work force, were included, the average weekly wage dropped to less than $4.00 a week because women were paid about $2.00 a week and children as little as twenty-five cents a week.[27] Rent was usually deducted from wages as well as any money owed at the company store. As profits increased and wages lagged behind because of the availability of immigrant labor, "an ever widening social gulf between master and workmen developed."[28]

Although the median wage was higher at the Cranston Print Works in comparison with the Sprague cotton mills, the Spragues paid no more than the going rate. Paternalism did not extend to paying higher wages. In fact, the Sprague Company had cut wages by 1857 so that they were paying less than other textile manufacturers. The Spragues also abused the company store price system, overcharging by as much as 25 percent. As a result, the workers went on strike in 1858, and the Sprague Company settled with the strikers, bringing wages up to the 1853 level and agreeing not to overcharge for goods at the company store.[29]

As long as the Spragues, following the general practice of other early mill owners, hired their workers mainly from the Yankee farm families in the neighboring villages, Spraguesville's population was largely homogeneous. But by the time the Protestant church was built for the mill workers in 1825, Spraguesville, in common with other mill communities in the state, had begun on a decade of expansion that changed Rhode Island's demography. Sprague and the other textile manufacturers began hiring Irish Catholic workers in the 1830s. In the 1835 census, a little over a thousand persons in the city of Providence were listed as "foreigners not naturalized," only about 5 percent of the total population but nonetheless a considerable and significant increase over the thirty-nine persons listed in the 1820 census. By 1842, the year of the Dorr Rebellion, the number of Catholics in the Providence parish had doubled to over two thousand. Practically all were of Irish descent.[30] Providence's population nearly doubled between 1840 and 1850, while Cranston's population increased by 50 percent during the same period, both increases largely due to the influx of Irish immigrants who were employed in the expanding textile industry.

The Providence River was the physical and social dividing line in antebellum Providence. The shipping and textile magnates built their hilltop mansions on the east side of the river near Brown University, where many of them served as trustees—the Allens, the Arnolds, the Browns, Sullivan Dorr (but not his son Thomas), the Durfees, the Hailes, the Iveses, old families all. The university itself in those days was a bastion of conservative philosophy, President Wayland and Professor William Goddard providing the religious and moral arguments for the conservative politicians and wealthy industrialists opposing Dorr's radical politics.

The Irish Catholic immigrants in the late 1830s and 1840s settled on the west side of the river, clustered around the Catholic church. This was the church the Gordons attended Sunday mornings, walking from Spraguesville; here were the rented tenements of friends the Gordons visited after mass, for Nicholas was a part of the Irish community in Providence as well as Cranston. Another Irish community, known locally as "Dogtown," developed in South Providence (still on the west side of the river) beginning in 1844, when cheap land for development of tenements became available between the factories near the river and the slaughterhouses further north.[31]

The population of Providence grew from 17,000 in 1830 to over 23,000 in 1840, a 35 percent increase due largely to Irish immigrants. By 1854, the Irish made up 20 percent of the total population of Providence, mostly concentrated on the west side of the river in one or the other of the two Irish neighborhoods. The Providence Irish community, living in ghettos, were physically isolated from the native-born population. Illiteracy and lack of skills further isolated them economically as they replaced better paid indigenous workers, working for lower pay. The native-born workers resented the immigrants, becoming suspicious of them as threats to their jobs. Furthermore, ill feeling between native and immigrant workers because of religious differences worsened the sense of social isolation. Nonetheless, although the Irish and their clergy were often harassed in Providence, there was no mob violence against them in

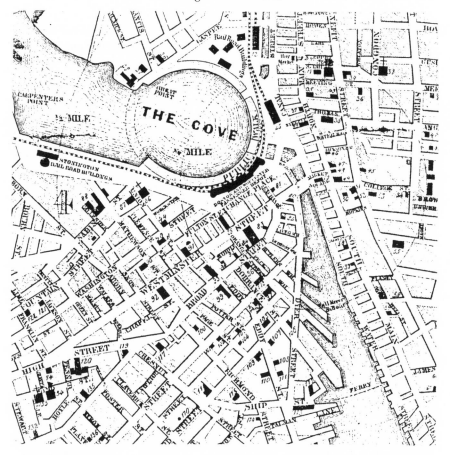

Detail of a map of Providence, 1849, showing the west side. Cushing and Walling, surveyors.

the 1830s and 1840s as there was in Boston and Philadelphia.[32] Possibly because of the discrimination against immigrants built into the Rhode Island constitution, the Irish were not seen as quite so direct a violent threat to the native-born population of Providence as they were in Boston and Philadelphia. Despite the anti-Catholic crusade of Henry B. Anthony, editor of the *Providence Journal,* there remained a vestige of the tradition of religious tolerance in the state going back to colonial times.

As early as 1834, a mob attacked the Ursuline Convent in Charlestown, Massachusetts, outside Boston. The convent was burned to the ground, although no lives were lost.[33] In 1844, a bloody riot in Philadelphia pitted Irish Catholics against native American Protestants. Forty people were killed and sixty were seriously wounded, a convent was burned to the ground, and other property, both public and private, was destroyed.[34] The following year (on July 4), the first national organization of nativism held its convention in the city of Brotherly Love.

Before 1838, Irish immigrants had tended to be from poor families, poor but not destitute, undereducated but not illiterate. Such in all probability was Nicholas Gordon's background, although somewhere along the line, whether in Ireland or the United States, he learned merchandising and storekeeping. But after the passage of the Irish Poor Law of 1838 in Great Britain, the typical Irish immigrants were more likely to be destitute and illiterate, for these were the ones the Anglo-Irish landlords, required to pay for the care of the poor under the new law, sent to America. On the whole, the Rhode Island Irish immigrants remained unskilled workers, belonging to a propertyless class.[35]

The hostility toward these immigrants, whether peasants or farmers, exhibited by the native population in Rhode Island had two sources: prejudice against them as foreigners of a different culture; and prejudice against them as Roman Catholics loyal to the pope. The two strands of intolerance came together in the warning of the political nativists that "the liberal suffrage clause of the People's Constitution would pave the way for the political ascendancy of those Irish Catholic immigrants who were swarming into the state in ever-increasing numbers."[36] It was in the context of these fears, inflamed by the recent arrest of Thomas Dorr for treason, that the Gordons found themselves accused of the murder of Amasa Sprague.

Amasa Sprague's standing in the community as its leading citizen was as much economic as it was social. The economic welfare of the village as a whole depended on the prosperity of the print works; even those not directly employed by the company—the tavern keepers, the farmers, the merchants—were indirectly dependent on the continuing success of the print works. Sprague's political influence in the town was an extension of his economic power, and the Cranston Town Council members were beholden to the Spragues directly or indirectly by reason of party politics or economic dependence. Sheldon Knight, for example, a mainstay of the council, belonged to the same political party as the Spragues and the Spragues would help elect him to the state legislature in April 1844, while Charles Searle, Sprague's agent, would be elected to the town council in the fall.

At the other end of the economic scale from the Spragues were the three younger Gordon brothers and their sister, Margaret, who had all arrived in Boston in late June or early July 1843. They were among the more than 65,000 immigrants who came from Ireland between 1841 and 1846.[37] They were poor; on the voyage to America John and William wore old shabby clothes, having nothing decent to wear until they were able to borrow something from their brother Nicholas. Like the vast majority of Irish immigrants, they were unskilled laborers. John worked as a laborer in the dye shop of the Drybrook mill in Johnston; Robert was a casual laborer, and even William who was identified as a tailor was, like many of his fellow immigrants in the trade, employed as an unskilled worker in a Providence tailor shop. Tailoring was the largest category of occupation among Irish workers in Boston, followed by common laborer and domestic servant.[38] In as much as their sister was employed as a domestic servant in Providence, the younger Gordons fitted into the three main categories of occupation among Irish immigrants. But even such humble, low-paying occupations were not always open to the Irish. Advertisements in Boston newspapers sometimes specified that "none need apply but Americans," thus preventing Irish immigrants from getting these domestic service jobs and condemning them to a life of poverty in the slums. And even though 2,000 Irish females did work as domestic servants in Boston in 1850 because the occupation was considered too menial for native Americans, some Boston newspaper ads specified that applicants for domestic service be Protestant foreigners, if not Americans.[39]

The Gordon siblings had one important advantage over most of their fellow immigrants who arrived in Boston in 1843: they had an older brother who paid their passage and met them when they arrived. And they had a home to go to when they reached Cranston. The typical penniless immigrant who landed in Boston or New York had "no alternative but to stay where he was." These destitute peasants from the south of Ireland constituted Boston's main immigrant population.[40] Such economic deprivation was evident among the immigrants in Rhode Island also, especially in Providence. In 1850, nearly one-half of the inmates in the Dexter Asylum poorhouse were Irish immigrants. These paupers— whether physically or mentally ill, alcoholics, old, "immoral" (prostitutes), wives deserted by their husbands, orphans or, as one unfortunate Irish adolescent of sixteen was designated, "deaf, Dumb, and friendless"— were all dumped together in the asylum. Yet they fared better than their fellow paupers in the Portsmouth (Rhode Island) poorhouse, where any inmate who broke a house rule was confined "to solitary confinement in a dungeon," there to be kept on bread and water "for as long as the keeper deemed necessary."[41]

Nicholas Gordon was more fortunate than his siblings when he arrived in this country in the mid-1830s, probably about 1836, and presumably in the port of Boston also. He either had sufficient capital at that time with which to begin his business or else had friends in Rhode Island from whom he could borrow. He was obviously the bright one in the family as well as the oldest son. He was certainly the most enterprising and ambitious of the four brothers. He settled first in Knightsville (sometimes called "Monkey Town"), where he set up a small store, probably in rented quarters. The store was about a mile down the road from the Cranston Print Works. In 1836 or 1837, Nicholas moved to Spraguesville and opened a general store selling groceries, notions, and candy in the immediate vicinity of the print works, not far from Amasa's house.

Nicholas Gordon kept in touch with Ireland through the members of his family still living there. He also kept up with Irish politics and was "an ardent Repealer."[42] Repeal of the Act of Union of England and Ireland, which had been passed in 1801, was as emotional an issue for Irish Americans in 1841 as union of the north and south of Ireland is today. Two rival Repeal associations were formed in Providence that same year, one headed by the antislavery reformer Patrick O'Connell and Dorrite Henry Duff, and the other by the conservative authoritarian priest and temperance leader, Father Corry. One can well assume that Gordon would have supported O'Connell and Duff, although it was Corry who prevailed in the end.[43]

The temperance society was one organization Nicholas Gordon would not have joined. The Irish Catholic community in Providence did not affiliate with the Protestant-dominated temperance society, preferring to organize their own group under the auspices of Father Corry. The Catholic society not only demanded abstinence "from all kinds of ardent spirits, strong beer, ale and porter except prescribed medicine," but also required those taking the pledge to actively discourage the sale of such spirits.[44]

Nicholas Gordon's store prospered in a small way, but he knew the selling of liquor would make it profitable. He had become part of the community by the spring of 1840, had learned the ins and outs of town politics, and felt confident enough to apply to the town council for a license to sell liquor and wine by the bottle in the store (but not by the drink, which was then called "keeping tavern"). To assure being granted the license, he convinced Jeremiah Carpenter, a forty-four-year-old carpenter and a member of the Cranston Town Council, to post bond for him.[45] Carpenter's influence with the town council was twofold—not only was he a member, but he was also Sprague's former brother-in-law, having married Susanna Sprague Mathewson after the death of her husband.[46] Carpenter was also a supporter of Dorr's People's Constitution, and voted to ratify it in 1841.[47] (In those days the Sprague brothers supported Thomas Dorr in his drive for suffrage reform.) With Carpenter's support Gordon was granted his license, and it was renewed the following April for another year. No complaint against Gordon was recorded either at the initial granting or at the time of renewal in the official records of the Cranston Town Council.[48]

By the spring of 1842 Gordon had prospered sufficiently to buy a $200 parcel of land on which he built a house and store.[49] He was by then a naturalized citizen, and the ownership of unencumbered real property worth more than $134 made him eligible to vote under the new constitution which would take effect the following year, but each town had the right to determine the qualifications of its own freemen.[50] He applied for the status of freeman at the Cranston Town Meeting in late August 1842. At the same town meeting at which Nicholas was officially granted the right to vote, Amasa Sprague was elected to represent Cranston in the Rhode Island General Assembly.[51]

In the fall of 1842, Nicholas Gordon was granted a license "to keep an Ale House at his store in this town [Cranston] and to retail therein in any

quantity (except on Sundays) wines and strong liquors." He was thus able
to sell liquor by the drink, a more profitable way of dispensing it to the
workers at the print works nearby. There is no record of any objection
being raised at the time of granting the license, and it was renewed on
April 3, 1843, the usual time for renewal, but only for three months, as
was true for all the liquor licenses approved at that time. The short term
of the renewal was mandated by an act of the General Assembly and does
not mean there was a complaint against Gordon.[52]

Around this time Gordon decided he could afford to send for the rest
of his family, paying for their passage to the United States—his three
brothers (John, William, and Robert), his mother, Ellen, his sister, Margaret, and William's seven year old daughter (William's wife having died).
Probably Nicholas used the services of his friend Jeremiah Baggott of
Providence, who had been appointed agent for the Joseph Murray company of New York, in April 1843. Baggott as agent engaged "to bring out
Passengers from all the principal towns in Ireland direct to Boston or by
way of New York. . . . Should the individuals sent for conclude not to
emigrate, the money will be refunded . . . after deducting 5 per cent for
postage and other expenses. He will also give drafts in sums to suit
applicants, payable in every town in Ireland, England and Scotland."[53]
Having sent for his family, Nicholas built an addition to the house to
provide room for them and to accommodate increased business.

Nicholas Gordon shared with the Spragues at least one characteristic—
a determination to succeed, make money, and accumulate property. He
was more the embodiment of the American dream of success than were
Amasa and William Sprague, who after all had inherited a thriving business from their father. Nicholas was a self-made man determined to rise
above the mass of poor Irish immigrants.

At the very moment of his dream's fulfillment, reunited with his family
in the early summer of 1843, his downfall began. The town council took
up the renewal of his liquor license in July 1843. Gordon no longer had
any supporter on the town council, Jeremiah Carpenter no longer being a
member. The council was completely dominated by Amasa Sprague's
political allies, and although Amasa had chosen not to stand for reelection
to the Rhode Island General Assembly in April 1843, the political control
he wielded in his own community remained strong. Pressured by Amasa
Sprague's agents, the town council voted unanimously in July 1843 to
deny the renewal of Nicholas Gordon's liquor license. His main source of

income immediately dried up. His ensuing quarrel with Amasa Sprague became the core of the prosecution's case against Nicholas Gordon for the murder of Amasa Sprague.

On March 27, 1844, the prosecution, led by the attorney general of Rhode Island, Joseph M. Blake, convinced the grand jury to return an indictment of murder and conspiracy to murder against the three Gordon brothers. Specifically, John and William and some person unknown were charged as principals and as being present, aiding, and abetting in the murder of Amasa Sprague. Nicholas was charged with abetting, hiring, procuring, stirring up, and moving John and William Gordon, and another person unknown, to perpetrate the crime of murder against Amasa Sprague. Trial was set for April 8 before the Rhode Island state supreme court.

CHAPTER THREE

The Prosecution

The trial was held in the original State House on North Main Street. A brick building built in 1762, it was the site of the Rhode Island General Assembly's declaration of independence from England on May 4, 1776. A wooden clock tower topped the front entrance which was originally set back from the street but was extensively changed in 1850 by the addition of an Italianate entrance reached by a steep stairway. Later an extension was built backing onto Benefit Street, its entrance not far from the Sullivan Dorr house on the other side of the street. The building itself still stands today, housing, among other state agencies, the offices of the State Historical Preservation Commission. Unfortunately, the interior has been greatly altered since the time of the Gordon trials.

Even before the trial could begin and the jury could be selected, there was legal maneuvering between the prosecution and defense counsels. Thomas F. Carpenter, acting for the defense, moved that each of the prisoners have a separate trial. The prosecution, led by State Attorney General Joseph M. Blake, raised no objection to a separate trial for Nicholas Gordon, who was charged with being an accessory to murder before the fact, but he objected to separate trials for John and William, who were charged with committing the murder. Chief Justice Job Durfee, speaking for the court, ruled that John and William must stand trial jointly. It was a ruling unfavorable to the defense, for it had been apparent from preliminary hearings that the prosecution case against John Gordon was stronger than that against his brother William.

This trial was no hole-in-the-corner affair. The Irish Catholic community in Providence had rallied to the support of the indicted Gordons, raising a substantial defense fund to hire able counsel.[1] The four presiding judges hearing the case were justices of the supreme court of Rhode

Island, and some of the best legal minds in the state acted as counsel for both sides.[2] Both lawyers and judges were leaders in Rhode Island politics, albeit on different sides. Thomas Carpenter, the leader of the defense team, had been an unsuccessful Democratic candidate for governor in 1840 and again in 1842. He had been one of the most influential supporters of Dorr's suffrage movement, and in the 1843 election, the first under the new constitution, he had run for governor as an "Equal Rights" Democrat; he had lost to the new Law and Order Party (a collection of conservative Whigs and Democrats) largely because of the defection of a number of conservative Democrats to the other side.[3] Samuel Y. Atwell, his associate, had run for the office of attorney general on the losing Democratic ticket in the election of 1843 and had been a prominent liberal Democrat in the state legislature and a member of the reformist Rhode Island Suffrage Association. In 1838 Atwell and supreme court justice William R. Staples published a report to the state legislature recommending the abolition of capital punishment.[4]

Rounding out the defense team were John P. Knowles and Samuel Currey who had acted for the Gordons during the hearing before the examining magistrate in January. Knowles was in the same law office as Carpenter, and like Carpenter and Atwell, had been a prominent supporter of Dorr. He, with Carpenter, Atwell, Dorr, and five other prominent Rhode Island lawyers, published in 1842 a defense of the people's right to form a new constitution based on Dorr's theory that the sovereign power of the state passed to the people by reason of the American Revolution.[5] Balancing the defense team's liberal, reformist composition was Currey, a conservative anti-Dorrite by reputation and a protégé of Albert C. Greene, serving his apprenticeship in Greene's law office.[6]

The head of the prosecution team, Attorney General Blake, had been, like Amasa Sprague, a conservative Democrat who joined the antisuffrage Whigs in the Law and Order Party. He was a strong legal opponent in a murder trial. In 1833 when he was only twenty-three years old, he served as part of the defense team in Rhode Island's previously most celebrated and important murder case, the trial of the Reverend Ephraim K. Avery charged with the murder of mill worker Sarah Maria Cornell. The defense won a verdict of not guilty in that case.[7] As chief prosecutor for the state in the Gordon case, Blake was seeking nothing less than a verdict of guilty of murder against all three Gordon brothers.

The influence of William Sprague was strongly represented at the very center of the prosecution's presentation. Blake's associate, a young Providence lawyer named William H. Potter, had been personally chosen by William Sprague. The junior partner in the law office of former Attorney General Albert C. Greene, Potter had no official standing in the government of the day. Since the attorney general had no assistants in those days, it was the customary practice for the court to permit an outside lawyer to assist the attorney general. In an important case involving a capital crime, the assistant would likely be a former attorney general, as was the case in the Avery trial.[8] What was extraordinary was the fact that William Sprague had been allowed to choose the assistant, although admittedly his first choice had been the former attorney general, Albert C. Greene. However unusual the arrangement, it was accepted both by the court and by the defense.

Potter was an eminently acceptable choice to Attorney General Blake, for he had all the required conservative credentials. His father had been a large landholder in the southern part of the state, conservative by conviction, and a member of the state legislature and the U.S. Congress. His brother Elisha followed their father into politics, serving in the state legislature, and was a friend and political ally of William Sprague. William Potter, a Phi Beta Kappa graduate of Brown University in 1836, had entered Harvard Law School for two years and then apprenticed in Albert Greene's law office. Both Elisha and William Potter had been active in the anti-Dorr movement; William had been a delegate to the conservative, anti-Dorr Landholders' Convention to frame a new constitution, and he had also served as an officer in the Providence Horse Guards, defending the state against Dorr's army in June 1842.[9]

The Carpenter-Atwell defense team and the Blake-Potter prosecution team were not only legal adversaries and members of opposing political parties, but three of the four of them had been contenders on opposite sides in a bitterly contested election less than a year before. The election of 1843 had been the Dorr war all over again. Voter intimidation and vote fraud "exceeded any seen before in the State."[10] It would seem reasonable that political antagonism and hard feelings would still be present, particularly on the losing Democratic side. But at the same time, all these men were part of an interrelated network of Rhode Island lawyers and judges who belonged, as it were, to the same club. The stage was set for a clash of social and political attitudes that were mainly unstated but were implicit in the situation of two immigrant Irishmen being tried for the murder of a wealthy mill owner and prominent anti-Dorrite. With the shadow of Dorr's trial for treason in two weeks' time hanging over the trial, political antagonisms were never very far beneath the surface, particularly since many of the same legal and judicial participants would be involved in the Dorr trial.

No greater adversary on constitutional theory could be found in the state to preside over Dorr's trial than Chief Justice Job Durfee, for he had already declared Dorr's actions treasonable. And no greater symbol of that social and cultural divide between the two Irish Catholic immigrants and the Protestant, old Rhode Island family elite could be found to preside over the Gordons' trial than Job Durfee. Graduate of Brown University, politician, lawyer, jurist, and sometime poet, his world was as distant from the Gordons as his epic poem, "What Cheer," published in 1832, was from what cheer the Gordons could find in the nearest tavern.[11]

With Judge Durfee's ruling that John and William Gordon were to be tried jointly, the trial was ready to proceed. The prisoners were arraigned and pleaded not guilty, and the selection of the jury began from the forty-three men drawn from the pool of eligible jurors in Providence County, consisting of nine townships, including Cranston where Amasa Sprague had lived and Johnston where he had died. Of the forty-three potential jurors, twenty-two were peremptorily challenged by the defense, John and William each being allowed eleven challenges. Of the remaining twenty-one, six were dismissed as having already formed or expressed an opinion as to the guilt or innocence of the accused. A final three were dismissed as having conscientious scruples of finding a man guilty of a crime punishable by death, leaving twelve men tried and true empanelled as the jury (*Trial*, 6).

As in the Avery case eleven years previously, the members of the jury were allowed to keep their own notes of the testimony. James C. Hidden, a Providence businessman and partner with his brother in an engraving and copperplate company was chosen foreman of the jury. Thomas Carpenter knew him well, having been a partner in the business until James Hidden bought him out. Furthermore, they had offices in the same building, and Carpenter would often discuss questions of law with Hidden, who had a keen legal mind although he was not a lawyer. However, there was no cause or excuse for complacency by Carpenter in the choice of Hidden as foreman. Hidden was a conservative Whig politician who had served in the state legislature and eventually became speaker of the

House of Representatives. He was also an anti-Dorrite, serving as a captain of the Fifth Ward City Guard during the Dorr Rebellion.[12] Coincidentally, the fifth ward of Providence included the area around the Catholic church where the Irish had settled.

The fact that all but the twelve jurors from the original forty-three had been challenged and dismissed for one reason or another turned out to be crucial. On the second day of the trial, after testimony had begun, one of the jurors asked to be excused from serving because he had learned his grandson was dying. The court excused him by joint consent of the prosecution and defense counsel. The defense counsel raised no objection to the proceedings nor did they raise any objection to the eleven remaining jurors being reempanelled and a twelfth juror, Jonah Steere, a drawn juror previously dismissed, being sworn in to make up the "new" jury.

The decision by defense counsel not to contest the reempanelling of the same jury (with the addition of a previously dismissed juror) was an inexplicable and serious error in judgment, for it was a missed opportunity to have John and William Gordon acquitted on appeal as constituting double jeopardy. This lack of an aggressive defense strategy at the beginning of the trial was detrimental to the best interests of the Gordons. The best that can be said for it is that Carpenter and his associates were not consciously derelict in their duty to their clients. Being politicians in a small state and part of an interrelated network of lawyers and judges who all knew each other, they had learned accommodation rather than aggressive confrontation within the legal and judicial system whatever their political differences. It was, as Charles Carroll suggests in *Rhode Island: Three Centuries of Democracy,* an illustration of "the easy-going practice in early trials," that the trial continued without objection being raised.[13] After all, in the Avery murder trial in 1833 the preliminary hearing was begun by supreme court justices Levi Haile (presiding at the Gordon trial) and John Howe before the defense team, including Joseph Blake, had been assembled, and before the assigned prosecutor, William Staples (in the absence of the attorney general), had been able to arrive in town.

Perhaps also, Samuel Atwell was already too ill at this early stage of the trial to have his full wits about him to raise the objection; certainly, by the end of the trial, Atwell, principal counsel for John and William Gordon, was unable to argue the petition for a new trial. The cause of his illness is not known, but it was serious enough for him to be bedridden.

Whatever the reason for not pursuing a more active defense of legal objection over the dismissal of a juror after the testimony had begun, the defense counsel accepted the form without the substance of a new trial, and John and William Gordon were again arraigned and again pleaded not guilty. The new juror, Jonah Steere, joined Asa Steere on the jury, together with George Whipple, a Providence hatter, and Lebbeus Whipple, the relationships in either case unknown. Given the large family clans that dominated the Yankee population of Rhode Island, it was inevitable that some of the names would be duplicated whatever the relationship. After all, several of the witnesses for the prosecution were named Sprague, and fourteen Carrs and twenty-four Shaws appeared in the 1850 Providence city directory, among them jurors Nicholas Carr (furniture manufacturer) and Joseph C. Shaw (blacksmith).

William Potter's opening statement for the prosecution followed the traditional pattern, outlining the government's case against the defendants. He summarized the evidence—the murder weapon, a gun, would be linked to the Gordon brothers; the tracks in the snow leading from the scene of the crime would be shown to lead to the Gordon house; a pair of boots belonging to John Gordon would be shown to fit these tracks; a coat found buried near the tracks would be identified as one belonging to Nicholas Gordon and worn by his brother John, and finally William Gordon would be identified by eyewitnesses who saw him near the scene of the crime with a gun before the time of the murder and again afterwards without the gun. Since the evidence was actually circumstantial, Potter emphasized that in law "facts may be proved by circumstantial testimony in a manner as strong and conclusive to the mind as by positive testimony" (*Trial*, 11).

Although only John and William Gordon were on trial, their brother Nicholas was at the center of the prosecution's case against the defendants. Potter specifically pointed out that Nicholas Gordon had been indicted as an accessory before the fact and charged with "instigating the prisoners to the commission of the deed." Once he established that in law Nicholas Gordon was a principal "equally guilty with him who gives the blow," Potter argued that Nicholas's alleged "feelings of the bitterest hostility" toward Amasa Sprague became John's and William's, by reason of being "expressed in the presence of the prisoners." Although neither John nor William knew of Amasa Sprague's existence before July 1843, Potter claimed that "they were moved by a hate long harbored; by a spirit of revenge which never forgot its object, and which the life of the victim, alone, could not satisfy" except by savagely beating him to death "upon God's holy Sabbath" (*Trial*, 7).

The government, Potter insisted, was emotionally neutral, its only motivation being the highest: to perform its duty and ascertain the truth and to protect the innocent and punish the guilty. Turning from the jury for a moment, Potter waved in the direction of William Sprague who was present in the courtroom attending to the progress of the trial. Senator Sprague, he assured the jury, desired only the truth and entertained no other feelings toward the prisoners than that their innocence or guilt be proved. Having asserted that both the government and the Spragues were without an ounce of prejudice, the prosecution was ready to present the case.

There was still time that first day of the trial to begin the testimony. Only the preliminary evidence was then presented, establishing the extent of the fatal wounds, the location of the scene of the crime, the last time Amasa Sprague was seen alive, the fact that he was in the habit of taking the same path every Sunday, and finally when and by whom the body was first discovered.

The evidence against the Gordons was introduced the second day of the trial. A small piece of a gun or pistol "with blood and hair" on it was found at the site of the crime. A single track in the snow led to the discovery of an old coat with "blood on it" hidden in the brush some distance from the murder scene. A gun, the murder weapon, was found near by. Tracks from the hiding places of the gun and coat led to the back door of the Gordon home. And finally, a pair of boots taken from the house seemed to fit the size of the footprints in the track. Later, other pieces of the gun were found at the murder site. All the physical evidence except the original piece of gun had been discovered *after* the arrest of the Gordons when the investigation had focused entirely on finding evidence against them. Consequently, other possible evidence had been neglected. For example, there were at least two other sets of tracks leading away from the murder scene that were never investigated.

Much of the early prosecution testimony concerning the discovery of clues and evidence was given by Walter Beattie. Beattie was a villager, a Sprague employee, who lived near the print works. He led a search party of villagers that included David Lawton, Luther Mason, and Nathan

Pratt. They were the ones who followed the first set of tracks and discovered the coat and the gun. Such was the close cooperation between the villagers and the county authorities in the gathering of evidence that the sheriff gave John Gordon's boots to Walter Beattie to keep in his possession.

A precedent did exist for such close cooperation between a citizens' vigilance committee, the Sprague family, and the sheriff's office in the gathering of evidence, as well as for William Sprague's actively aiding the prosecution in its preparation and presentation of the case. In the Avery murder trial of 1833 an investigating committee of private citizens representing the cotton manufacturing industry had been deeply involved in gathering evidence for the sheriff and in helping the attorney general of Rhode Island prepare for the trial. Even after the trial began, the committee continued its investigations.[14]

At the center of the circumstantial evidence against John and William Gordon was the murder weapon. Blake could not prove that either William or John Gordon owned a gun, but he had evidence to show that one N. Gorton had purchased a gun in October 1843. Alfred Wright, an agent for the Delaware & Hudson Coal Company in Providence, traced the gun that Nicholas Gordon had purchased. If this gun proved to be the murder weapon, it would be damning evidence against the Gordons. Testimony about the gun came out almost inadvertently when Samuel Atwell for the defense cross-examined Gardner Luther. Luther, a fifty-nine-year-old native of Rhode Island, lived in Cranston at the time and was probably working in the print works. He had testified to the fact that he had found small pieces of a gun at the murder site on Wednesday, three days after the murder—a gun cock, the tube of a percussion lock, and a screw head. Atwell was attempting to disassociate Nicholas from the gun by gaining an admission from a prosecution witness that the gun was not Gordon's. Luther admitted he did not know "that Nicholas Gordon ever had this gun." But, he continued, "I have seen him with a gun. I think it was two weeks previous to the murder. Can't say whether the gun resembled the gun in Court or not" (*Trial*, 24).

The damage had been done, and Attorney General Blake, undoubtedly smiling inwardly, saw his opening: "Did you know of Nicholas Gorden [*sic*] having a gun about the time of the murder?" Before the witness could answer, Samuel Atwell rose to object to the attorney general's question: "It has nothing to do with the guilt or innocence of these men whether

Nicholas Gordon owned a gun or not. The Government must first prove that the gun was ever in the hands of these prisoners. Nicholas Gordon is not now on trial. The prisoners must be brought in contact with the gun."

Blake countered with the argument that the murder had "undoubtedly" been committed with that gun, and that it was permissible for the prosecution to prove the ownership of the murder weapon in order to show that "the prisoners might have access to it." Atwell insisted that the prosecution first needed to establish that the prisoners had had contact with the gun before seeking to prove whose gun it was. Chief Justice Durfee, however, ruled in favor of the prosecution (*Trial*, 24).

The ruling was a serious blow to the defense, for the prosecution could now slant the case as though Nicholas Gordon were on trial with William and John, and it was free to imply that the gun was Nicholas's and that William and John had used it to murder Amasa Sprague at Nicholas's command. The next several witnesses connected Nicholas Gordon, and by inference his two brothers, to the gun.

One of the witnesses who unequivocally stated that the murder weapon, or at least part of it, belonged to Nicholas Gordon was Benjamin Waterman, known locally as Ben Kit. Described as "a kind of simple man," his testimony was direct:

> Ben Kit: It [the ramrod of the murder weapon] belonged to Nicholas Gordon. . . . I know the ramrod, sir. I should know it the darkest night ever was seen—tell it by feeling, sir. It was the week before New Years.
> Attorney General: What year?
> Ben Kit: Don't know the year, sir. Don't keep the run of the years. Can't write nor cipher. Make my mark, sir—that's all. (*Trial*, 33–34)

John Gordon was linked to the murder weapon by prosecution witness Abner Sprague, Jr. Abner was a cousin of Amasa Sprague, and his family's farm, inherited from their mutual grandfather, William Sprague, was near the murder site. Together with his wife, Amy, Abner owned property valued at over $12,000 in 1850, a considerable sum considering that the whole of the Cranston Print Works was then evaluated at $110,000. He testified that he had seen John Gordon with a gun near the scene of the crime two days before the murder, and that when he later saw the murder weapon he was convinced it was the same gun: "I thought it the same gun I saw John Gordon have; I have no doubt of it at all; I said at the time I thought it was John Gordon's gun. It was all bloody then" (*Trial*, 31).

This was damaging testimony, and on cross-examination Atwell could not shake his story. The best he could do was to get Abner to admit that he could not "say positively this is the gun I saw John Gordon have," but he repeated he had "no manner of doubt it is the same." He denied he knew either William or John Gordon had been arrested by the time the gun was found; in other words, that he had leaped to the conclusion it was the same gun because he knew the Gordons had been arrested for the murder. That he would not have known of the arrest is difficult to believe since the Abner Sprague farm house was the only house between the murder scene and Nicholas Gordon's house in the village. Certainly Abner Sprague, Jr., would have been right there with all the others searching for evidence the next morning and would have heard of the Gordons' arrest, given the way news spreads in a village. The Abner Spragues were not disinterested spectators, being cousins of Amasa Sprague. Abner Sprague, Sr., was the last man to see Amasa alive, according to his own testimony.

Since it was the murder weapon, the gun was the most important single piece of evidence the prosecution possessed, and it was vital to the prosecution's case to link the defendants to it, however circumstantial the testimony. Even before the testimony of Abner Sprague, Jr., the prosecution had carefully identified the murder weapon as the secondhand fowling piece Nicholas Gordon had purchased in the fall of 1843 at an auction in Tillinghast Almy's store in Providence. The previous owner of the gun, James Francis, a black man, positively identified the murder weapon as the gun he had left with Almy to sell: "This is the gun, I should know it among a dozen. . . . I would swear my life upon it" (*Trial*, 27). Atwell attempted to discredit the evidence because the sales entry in Almy's book was to an N. Gorton, not Gordon, but Almy insisted that N. Gorton and Nicholas Gordon were one and the same person, recalling that Nicholas had "laughed at me for my Yankee manner of spelling his name" (*Trial*, 28).

In an attempt to link both William and John Gordon to a gun on the day of the murder, Blake called William Barker and Bowen Spencer, Providence residents visiting in Cranston on the day Sprague was killed. They testified that they had met a tall man and a short man with a gun on the Plainfield Turnpike just north of the murder scene no later than two o'clock, a couple of hours before the murder. They again met the same two men on the same road at sunset, shortly after the time of the murder. The tall man was now carrying the gun and the short man was without his coat, despite the cold. Both Barker and Spencer later identified the short man as William Gordon, although neither of them had ever met him or the two men before. William was short, apparently about the same height as the short man, but although John was taller, he did not fit the description of the tall man. Neither of the two witnesses identified the tall man.

Second in importance to the gun as evidence was the bloodstained coat found hidden in the brush near the spot where the murder weapon had been discovered. Attorney General Blake was determined to connect the bloodstained coat to the Gordons, for the coat had a hole in the right elbow and blood had soaked into the white lining, and when the Gordon house was searched a shirt had been found "which, on the elbow, had a stain of the appearance of blood on it, or blood and water" (*Trial*, 27). A pair of boots was also found in the search of the house. Although the boots fit the prints in the snow, they were "common sale boots," and many men owned boots like them, whereas the coat was distinctive. Earlier testimony had been inconclusive as to whether the coat found near the hidden gun was indeed the same old coat Nicholas had had in his possession many months before, but the testimony established in the minds of the jury the fact that Nicholas owned a similar coat at one time and that when the house was searched the coat, like the gun, was not on the premises.

But before the connection with the coat could be made, Blake needed to establish firmly the prosecution's theory that the crime was a conspiracy between Nicholas and his brothers based on Nicholas Gordon's hatred of Amasa Sprague. He questioned Richard Knight, who, acting on Sprague's instructions, had objected to the renewal of Nicholas's liquor license: "Do you know of Nicholas Gordon having any difficulty with Amasa Sprague?" This time the defense counsel was prepared to object and Thomas Carpenter rose, arguing at length against admission of Knight's testimony which he knew would provide the opening the prosecution needed in order to present the details of the conspiracy and its motivation.

Carpenter argued that it was presumptive to infer that John and William Gordon shared any yet unproved hostility toward Amasa Sprague, and that it was a further presumption to infer that John and William would be motivated thereby to commit murder. William Potter argued that the government had already proved conspiracy: "A conspiracy need not be proved by the declaration of the persons forming it. It may be proved by the acts of the persons engaged in it," and that a prima facie case of conspiracy has already been established in the trial, Attorney General Blake argued further that it was common sense to prove motivation and that since a prima facie case of conspiracy had already been established, "the declaration of one of the conspirators now on trial may be offered against the others" (*Trial*, 36, 37). At this point Atwell for the defense objected to the admission of such testimony: Nicholas Gordon was not now on trial with the other two. After some deliberation during the noon recess, the justices again ruled in favor of the prosecution, stipulating only that any evidence presented regarding threats made by Nicholas against Amasa must be confined to proof of hostility made in the presence of William and/or John (*Trial*, 41). It was, to say the least, an unprecedented decision by the court and a fatal blow to the defense strategy. As one observer of the court stated, "the decision of the Supreme Court that threats made by another person in the presence of an accused prisoner are admissible as tending to prove a motive on the latter's part, without actual proof of a conspiracy or an effective response, stands unique in the annals of American criminal trials." The decision never became a precedent in any later trial.[15]

The defense raised one more objection before the prosecution swore in Miss Susan Field, its final major witness. This came in response to Blake's attempt to reinforce his conspiracy theory by establishing that Nicholas did *not* commit the act of murder on that fateful Sunday, implying that he had deliberately provided himself with an alibi by staying in Providence and had left his two brothers to murder Amasa. Chief Justice Durfee ruled that the evidence was admissible. Only one time during the prosecution's case had the court made a ruling favorable to the defense, and that was when Blake had tried to present testimony showing "hostile feeling and bitter enmity on the part of Nicholas S. Gordon towards the deceased" not made in the presence of William and John Gordon. The court ruled such testimony inadmissible (*Trial*, 46).

Susan Field's testimony against the Gordons was very damaging. Other witnesses had testified to bits and pieces of the mosaic of circumstantial evidence against the Gordons, but she pulled it all together, almost as though she had been rehearsed in her role of choric summation. She said that she had known Nicholas for three years, from the time she had first gone to live with her mother in Cranston, and had visited his store frequently, "as often as three times a week." She had known William and John, she said, since their arrival in July. When the bloodstained coat found in the swamp was shown to her, she identified it as the old blue coat belonging to Nicholas. She identified various pieces of clothing found in Gordon's house during the search, but not specifically the shirt with the alleged blood stains on the elbow; yet she left the impression that all the clothing belonged to one or another of the brothers, except for a very old and ill-shaped hat that she had never seen before. The main significance of her testimony about the clothing was that it established William and John owned few clothes of their own and that Nicholas allowed them to wear his: "John and William had nothing decent until they began to wear Nick's clothes" (*Trial,* 43).

The ordinariness and the domestic everyday details of her testimony made it seem convincing, so that when she identified the coat as the same one Nicholas's dog slept on and was also worn by John, her testimony was believable. She testified that she had seen a gun and a pistol with a percussion lock in Nicholas's store, but she was not asked by the prosecution to identify the gun or pistol found near or at the scene of the crime.[16] Her most damaging testimony provided just what the prosecution wanted, evidence of Nicholas's threats against Sprague made in the presence of at least one of his accused brothers:

> I heard Nicholas say Amasa Sprague had taken his license away from him; he would be the death of him. They took John Holloway's license from him, God damn him, he shan't take mine away. I'll have my revenge. I'll be the death of him. John was present and an Irishman [unidentified] when this was said. The Irishman said, No, Nick, you don't mean so. Nicholas said, Yes, by God, I do mean so. I would run him through just as quick as I can wink, and he struck his fists together. Nicholas was head of the family. The rest did as he said. (*Trial,* 43–44)

The weakest part of the prosecution's argument was that John and William would commit murder for him simply because he asked them to. Not even Susan Field testified that he actually told them to do so, but the implication was there for the jurors to ponder.

Blake took a calculated risk in presenting Susan Field's testimony because she would be a vulnerable witness upon cross-examination. Samuel Atwell for the defense immediately went on the attack:

Q. Where do you live?
A. I live at No. 20 Benefit [Providence].

To live on Benefit Street today is to live on "a mile of history" among restored mansions, luxury condos, and gentrified homes. To live at 20 Benefit Street in 1844 was to live in a whorehouse serving the sailors who arrived on the ships docked in the Providence River below. How many of the jurors knew this is unknown, but certainly Justice William Staples could not help being aware of it; he lived at 75 Benefit Street, a block or two away. His birthplace, 52 Benefit Street, the Samuel Staples house, which still stands today, was even closer.

The attorneys and the justices would presumably be aware of the double-edged meaning of the address. To reinforce what living at 20 Benefit Street implied about Susan Field's reputation and character, Atwell pressed the point:

Q. Whom do you live with?
A. With Mrs. Susan P. Garner.
Q. Was not Mrs. Susan P. Garner formerly known as Susan Parr?
A. Her name is Mrs. Susan P. Garner; I have nothing to do with any other name.
Q. Was she not called Susan Parr?
A. I have told you her name once, and shan't tell it again.

Whatever respectability the name of Mrs. Garner may have afforded, the notoriety of Susan Parr as the madam of a whorehouse was evident, an implication that would not have escaped at least some of the jurors.

Atwell could not shake Susan Field's testimony against the Gordons. But he did undermine her supposed familiarity with the Gordon household and the number of times she was in their presence the summer John and William had arrived in Spraguesville. Her testimony about the clothes and who wore what left the impression that she was practically part of the household, but she admitted that she had been ill in August and had gone to Nicholas's store only about ten times that month. By the end of August she had moved to Providence and never went back to visit her mother, let alone the Gordons.

Almost matter-of-factly, Atwell asked:

Q. You know William and John, do you not?
A. I know them when I see them.
Q. There they both are [he paused dramatically, pointing to the accused]; which is William, and which John?

44

A. [Witness turns, points to William]. That is the one I am not so well acquainted with, that is John; that one [pointing to John] is William. (*Trial*,
45)

Atwell must have looked pleased as the jurors gasped at her blunder.
With a dismissing wave of the hand, he said to Susan Field, "There, you
may go now." Attorney General Blake attempted to salvage the situation
as best he could: "Miss Field, which is the one that tended the store?" She
answered, pointing to John, "This is the one." She was correct this time,
for if William is not John, then the other must be. Undoubtedly, the jury
would remember her mistaking William for John and John for William,
but they would also remember her vivid description of Nicholas Gordon's
threats against Amasa Sprague.

To leave the jury with the idea of Nicholas Gordon's passionate hatred
of Amasa Sprague, Blake closed his case with several witnesses to prove
that Amasa Sprague did in fact oppose the granting of a liquor license to
Nicholas Gordon in July. Despite the court's ruling that any expression of
Nicholas's hostility and enmity toward Sprague in the absence of John and
William Gordon was inadmissible evidence, it permitted testimony to
show a cause of hostility toward Sprague in the Gordon family "as an
independent act" without the prisoners having to be present (*Trial*, 46–
47). Thus the prosecution was able to bring in testimony dealing with the
denial of Nicholas's liquor license during the town council meeting in July.
The witness, Charles P. Searle, testified that Amasa opposed the license
before the council. Town council minutes for that date do not mention
Amasa Sprague by name. Only Searle's name is officially on the record as
opposing. However, a petition (or remonstrance) against granting the
license, "signed by a number of persons," was presented to the council at
the same time. As soon as the license was denied, permission was granted
to withdraw the petition as though it had never been made.[17]

Blake had what he wanted, direct testimony of the *act* motivating Nicholas Gordon to allegedly conspire with his brothers to murder Amasa
Sprague, as well as the *expression* of threats in the presence of John
Gordon. He had succeeded in trying Nicholas Gordon, the one brother
who was not on trial. In exasperation at the court's favoritism toward the
prosecution, particularly on this crucial question of motivation, Atwell
turned to Chief Justice Durfee: "We propose now, under the last ruling of
the court, to summon witnesses to prove that Mr. Sprague had had

difficulties with others; and, also, to show that they had an opportunity to commit this murder." In the tone of his answer Chief Justice Durfee again revealed his bias against the defense: "Well, sir, you can offer such evidence as you deem expedient, and if the court think it competent, they can suffer it to pass to the jury" (*Trial*, 47). Since Atwell did not actually produce any such witnesses and did not intend to, the offer was made sarcastically, and Durfee's reply was in kind.

Pressing his advantage over Atwell in this ruling by the court, Potter, attacked Nicholas Gordon in his closing argument:

> We prove the existence of feelings of hostility between one of the brothers, Nicholas, and the deceased. We show the cause of that hostility. It arose out of a fact which we calculated to produce bitter and revengeful feelings. It was an injury inflicted in that point where men are most susceptible. The deceased had been the means of preventing Nicholas S. Gordon obtaining a license, and by that means deprive him of a part of his gains. It was taking so much out of his pocket; thereby giving him the strongest motive for the commission of this act. In accordance with these facts, we find this man entertaining towards the deceased feelings of the direct hatred and revenge. . . . expressed repeatedly in the presence of the prisoners, accompanied by the most vindictive threats against the life of the deceased. (*Trial*, 48–49)

Potter summarized the evidence given by the witnesses against the three brothers, emphasizing for the jury, as he had in his opening statement, the visually tangible evidence rather than the circumstantial web of testimony. What was different from the opening statement was the focus he placed on the guilt of John Gordon, pointing to him as "the man who did this deed." The State's case against William Gordon was obviously weak by comparison, even in the context of the prosecution's testimony against him. The defense was quick to separate John from William in presenting its case.

CHAPTER FOUR

The Defense

Thomas Carpenter had been born and raised in the town of Cranston, and thus knew Spraguesville. Of average height, he nonetheless was a striking figure in the courtroom. His "very large head" dominated his appearance. He dressed in "a blue coat with brass buttons, black pantaloons, black satin vest, ruffled shirt, and black cravat." He could carry it off because "his manners were dignified but affable." When arguing a point, "his manner of speaking was formal and precise" rather than witty or rhetorical, "but he knew exactly what to say to a Rhode Island jury and a Rhode Island Court."[1] He presented a sharp contrast to the attorney general, who dressed conservatively as befitted his office as chief prosecutor for the state.

Carpenter's associate, Samuel Atwell, was an imposing figure in the courtroom. He gave the appearance of "a great, strong, burly man with a presence as powerful as that of Mr. [Daniel] Webster. He always dressed in black and spoke with great dignity and earnestness. . . . His power over a jury was wonderful, and his eloquence was heightened by a voice of peculiar magnetic properties."[2] The third member of the defense team was Samuel Currey, who, like Blake and Potter, presented an appropriately sober appearance as befitted his conservative politics; also he was a licensed Calvinist preacher as well as a practicing lawyer. But it had not always been that way: in his apprenticeship day he had the reputation of being "a bit of a dandy," parting his hair in the middle and wearing "a blue coat with brass buttons" and "a buff vest and yellow kid gloves."[3]

The fourth and final member of the defense team, John Power Knowles, was equally at ease in the world of the printed word and the law. He came from a poor family so that at age eleven he had to leave the Providence public school system and apprentice to a printer. He did so well that he became a master printer before he was twenty-one. Yet, in 1830, at age twenty-two, he gave it all up to study the law, graduating from Brown University in 1836 and Harvard Law School in 1838. In 1845, he was appointed master in chancery by the same supreme court justices he faced in the Gordon trial.[4] As master in chancery he was an officer of the court who assisted the justices in researching and reporting on matters of law and fact. In this capacity, and later as official reporter for the supreme court, he was able to combine his knowledge of the law with his mastery of the printed word. It was his role in the Gordon trial to research the law and the facts for the defense.

In his opening argument for the defense, Thomas Carpenter proposed an alternative theory that the two men, one tall and one short, whom the prosecution witnesses Barker and Spencer had met on the Plainfield Turnpike near the scene of the crime, "were the real murderers of Amasa Sprague" (*Trial,* 55). Since Barker and Spencer had both identified the short man as William Gordon (but not the tall man as his brother John), the defense needed to prove that the short man could not possibly have been William because he was elsewhere at the time, and that it was therefore a case of mistaken identity. Carpenter also proposed to prove that John Gordon was out of Spraguesville until the late afternoon, offering "such evidence as would satisfy the jury that John Gordon could not have committed that murder" (*Trial,* 55).

Witness after witness testified to seeing or being with William Gordon in the city of Providence that Sunday until well into the afternoon. Martin Quick testified he met William on a Providence street at about 3:00 P.M. William, who lived in Providence, was on his way to visit his sick mother in Spraguesville, and Martin was going back to his boardinghouse in Providence on Knight Street, running north from the Cranston road. William, convinced it was too cold to walk all the way to Spraguesville without fortifying himself, offered to stand Martin to a drink. It was only in the fourth tavern (admittedly on the way to Cranston) that they were able to be served a drink on Sunday. They parted company sometime between 3:00 P.M. and 3:30 P.M. (*Trial,* 57–58). As was true about most of the testimony, the time was not precise. Martin Quick at one point in his testimony stated he had left William at 3:00 P.M.; at another point in the same testimony, he placed the time as closer to 3:30 P.M.

The defense witnesses—Jeremiah Baggott, Michael Holohan, Jeremiah Ryan, Michael O'Brien, Catherine Holohan, Dennis O'Brien, John Gleason, Martin Quick, and Thompson Kingston—were all Irish, all Catholic. The nearest Catholic church the Gordons could attend was in Providence, and all three brothers could be expected to be in Providence Sunday morning, attending mass (their mother was too ill to go that day). It was their usual custom to visit with their friends among the Providence Irish Catholic community in the afternoon. Jeremiah Baggott's house, for example, was on Broad Street, the house next to the church. Jeremiah Ryan testified that William came to the house with Michael O'Brien between one and two o'clock "to the best of my belief." Since few watches were owned by the Irish poor, the times testified to were usually approximate. William stayed for dinner and left about an hour later. Nicholas came in soon after William had left, but it was some time before someone asked the hour. Any watch owned by an Irishman, no matter how cheaply made, was as much a status symbol as the gold watch worn by Amasa Sprague on the day of the murder. Nicholas Gordon, as a man of some property, owned a watch: he "drew out his watch, and said it was near 3 o'clock" (*Trial*, 57).

The testimony establishing William's alibi took up the entire morning session of Friday, April 12. Blake carefully cross-examined each of the witnesses, particularly Michael O'Brien, who had originally been arrested along with the Gordon brothers because he "was seen in company with the Gordons on Sunday [the day of the murder], and was known to have had a difficulty with Mr. Sprague."[5] As with the other witnesses, O'Brien was cross-examined about precise times:

Q. [Attorney General] How long did William Gordon stay after dinner [at the Holohans]?
A. Can't tell.
Q. Was it five minutes or twenty minutes?
A. Might be five, might be twenty; can't tell; he stopped about an hour in all. (*Trial*, 58)

Attorney General Blake sought to raise doubts about the character and bias of Michael O'Brien.

Q. You had heard of Mr. Sprague's murder, had you not?
A. Yes.

Q. Was nothing said about it [at Nicholas Gordon's house Sunday night]?
A. I don't recollect we did; I to Nicholas or he to me.
Q. Where were you when you first heard of Mr. Sprague's murder?
A. At a tavern near Hoyle tavern. . . .
Q. What was the first thing you said after hearing of the murder?
A. I don't know; I believe the first thing I said was to ask for something to
drink.

There was probably laughter in the courtroom at the answer. Then
sternly resuming his questioning, Blake asked O'Brien:

Q. Did you say nothing about the murder?
A. I can't recollect that I did.
Q. Do you recollect saying you were "damn glad of it," or any similar ex-
pression?
A. I don't know that I said so; can't recollect any thing about it.

The best Blake could do was to leave the implication that the vagueness
of O'Brien's memory was due to his having had too much to drink:

Q. You knew Mr. Amasa Sprague, did you not?
A. I did.
Q. You had worked for him, had you not?
A. Yes, worked for him four or five years.
Q. And you heard of him being murdered and said nothing about it, made
no remark?
A. I don't recollect saying anything about it; I had drunk considerable; I
was able to walk, but had as much as I could carry. (*Trial*, 58–59)

Over the weekend a surprise witness showed up for the defense. Actually, he was a missing witness, because William Gordon had insisted all
along that after he left Martin Quick he had met a man, an Irishman who
knew Nicholas but not him, on the road to Cranston that Sunday afternoon. The witness, Joseph Cole, boarded at Richard Knight's house,
having had the promise of work from Amasa. He and William had walked
together to Spraguesville, arriving at Richard Knight's house "within a
quarter of an hour of sun down." Since Knight's house was near the
Sprague mansion, it was not possible for William also to have been at the
footbridge helping to murder Amasa or to have been the short man seen

by Barker and Spencer. Once they reached Knight's house, "William asked me to come along to his [i.e., Nicholas's] house. I said no; it is against the law. By that I meant that Mr. Sprague had forbidden the workmen to go to Gordon's store; and if I went there should not get any work." As it turned out, he did not get work at the print works after all, and he left shortly thereafter for a job in New Jersey (*Trial*, 72).

Blake tried hard to discredit Joseph Cole's testimony both by cross-examining him sharply and by recalling Richard Knight as a witness. Left to stand unchallenged, Cole's testimony would effectively destroy Barker's and Spencer's identification of William as the short man seen by them shortly before and after the murder. Yet despite his obvious deference to authority and occasional contradictory statements on minor points, Cole did not waver on the main point of his evidence. Even his deference to authority explained why he had not come forward before to tell what he knew, even though he had been at the trial on the first day for a brief time:

Q. Why did you not communicate this fact at that time [at the very beginning of the trial as the indictment was being read]?
A. I thought I had once told it to Mr. Knight; he knew me, he was a competent man, and he would call me forward if it was important (*Trial*, 73).

Richard Knight had been a witness for the prosecution and had acted in a semiofficial capacity in gathering evidence against the Gordons. Knight's bias could be inferred from the fact that he was employed by the Spragues and had acted under orders from Amasa Sprague to appear in person with Charles Searle the previous summer at the town council meeting to object to granting Nicholas Gordon a liquor license. If Cole's story was true, Knight had held back vital evidence from the defense.

The attorney general attempted to place the onus on the witness, pressing the point that Joseph Cole had said nothing to anyone about what he knew at the beginning of the trial:

Q. Why did you not tell about it?
A. I thought the man who walked with me [William Gordon] had been discharged.
Q. Did you think William Gordon was discharged, after you came into the court room?
A. I did.

The legal maneuvering and the legal language of the indictment would have meant little to Joseph Cole, casual laborer.

Q. Who told you William Gordon was at liberty?
A. I understood it from Mr. Knight; this was when sitting at table at dinner, on Tuesday [January 2, 1844]. I thought from what Knight told me, the man I saw on the road, the tailor [William Gordon] was set at liberty. I don't know that Mr. Knight said so, but he took it so calm, I judged so from his manner. (*Trial*, 73)

Cole thought he had had momentous information to impart to Richard Knight, and since Knight had taken it so calmly, Cole concluded that William Gordon was already a free man and in no danger of being tried for murder. But Knight was a Yankee from an old family, and he had no respect for Irish laborers like Joseph Cole, who had been discharged from the print works two or three times in the past. Confident that the evidence against the Gordons was already overwhelming, Knight dismissed Cole's story as an attempt by a common laborer to appear important and at the same time help William Gordon, a fellow countryman.

Vital evidence favorable to the Gordons was deliberately withheld by Knight. It was also evident that evidence raising doubts as to the guilt of the Gordons was not followed up, whether it was a matter of tracks leading elsewhere than to the Gordon house or alternative identities for the tall man and the short man seen by Barker and Spencer. In his testimony for the prosecution on recall, Richard Knight denied he had ever had a conversation with Joseph Cole. Richard Knight revealed in his testimony the reason for his withholding information: "It was our policy [by the central committee of the vigilance committee] to keep everything secret, for the purpose of discovery" (*Trial*, 76).

John Cole, Joseph's brother, corroborated that his brother had left the house on the Sunday of the murder to go to Mr. Knight's boardinghouse in Spraguesville. A few days later, discussing the murder, John told Joseph that he thought the Gordons, by then arrested for the murder, were guilty. Joseph denied this could be true, saying he "walked with one of them, and could clear him." John Cole later told Jeremiah Baggott who said Joseph "is the very man we are looking for; we have searched for him" (*Trial*, 74–75). But by then Joseph had left for New Jersey, unable to obtain work at the Sprague print works. He returned to Providence sometime late in March, but it was not until the weekend of April 13 that defense counsel interviewed him and arranged for him to testify on the following Monday. John Cole was not cross-examined by Blake who counted on Knight's rebuttal testimony to counteract the effect of Joseph Cole's evidence. If the testimony of an Irish common laborer like Joseph Cole could be used by the defense to give an alibi to an Irish immigrant, the contradictory testimony of a Yankee could be used to weaken it. Then it remains to be seen whom the jury believes—Barker, Spencer, and Knight or O'Brien, Quick, and Cole.

The circumstantial evidence against John Gordon, however, was much stronger than that against William. But like an awaited absent character in the drama who never arrived but was central to it, Nicholas Gordon was essential to the prosecution's conspiracy theory. Consequently, the defense's strategy was to prove John innocent by proving Nicholas innocent. Witness after witness was called by the defense to prove that Nicholas did not own the old coat found near the scene of the crime and used in evidence against John. It is difficult, however, to prove a negative, as was shown in the testimony of Tillinghast Almy about the coat: "I never saw the coat exhibited here on Nicholas Gordon, to my knowledge." Since Almy was the prosecution witness who testified he had sold a gun to Nicholas Gordon, his testimony about the coat should have added weight. But the more he testified the less sure he seemed: "I don't know but I had as good an opportunity to see Nicholas Gordon as George Beverly had." Beverly was the clerk in the store who had often waited on Nicholas and had positively identified the coat as belonging to him. By the time Almy was cross-examined, he was reinforcing the prosecution's case: "I think Mr. Beverly is an observing man; that he would notice a man's coat sooner than I should" (*Trial*, 61). Later, on recall, Beverly reversed his testimony that it was the same coat Nicholas wore.

Several more witnesses followed, and all positively stated they had never seen Nicholas Gordon with such a coat. Similarly, the defense counsel called several other witnesses to interpret differently the circumstantial evidence brought against John Gordon. Why were his clothes and his boots wet when the house was searched upon his arrest? The prosecution insisted he wore them on the day of the murder, having waded in the swamp to hide the gun and coat, just as the bruise on his face was evidence of his struggling with Amasa Sprague. The wet boots and clothes, and the bruise, insisted the defense witnesses, including John's sister Margaret, were the result of a fall in the snow on Christmas Day. This is what John himself had said when he was arrested. He had been hesitant and reluctant to say so at first, he said, not because he was making up a story but because he would have had to admit he had been so drunk that day he couldn't stay on his feet.

The boots were damaging circumstantial evidence not just because they were wet but also because they fitted the imprints in the track. Atwell attempted to counteract the prosecution's evidence by producing a witness, John O'Brien, who had made his own measurement of the boot prints: "They are larger than John Gordon's boots," he stated positively. The measure presented by O'Brien in evidence was a piece of shingle supposedly the same length as John's boots, but on cross-examination Blake completely demolished O'Brien's testimony. The shingle O'Brien presented in evidence was not even the same piece of wood he had used to measure the tracks; furthermore, the shingle he produced as evidence was only a crude approximation of the original piece of wood, for he had measured the length by using his thumb. Finally, the two witnesses he said watched him measure the tracks denied he ever did so in their presence (*Trial*, 63, 69–71).

An important witness in John Gordon's defense was his mother. Ellen Gordon was the only person who could give him an alibi for the time of the murder. Relying on a mother's testimony for an alibi is always of doubtful value for the defense, but in this case it was doubly dangerous. Mrs. Gordon, according to the prosecution, had made damaging admissions about her son John on the day he was arrested, but since her testimony was vital to the defense, the attorneys took a calculated risk that her testimony under oath at the trial would outweigh anything she might have said in the confusion and stress of the day of the arrests, when she herself had been hauled off to prison.

Her testimony was that her son John had come home, she thought, about 2:00 P.M. that Sunday afternoon and did not leave the house until nearly 4:00 P.M. These times were only rough estimates, for having no clock, she could only tell the time by the sun, and the sun "was pretty low when he went out." He did not come back until after 7:00 P.M. The times of these comings and going were important because John had no other alibi for the period approximately between 3:30, when Amasa Sprague was last seen alive and approximately 4:30, when his body was discovered. Upon cross-examination Mrs. Gordon was asked by Blake:

Q. After he first came home, did he not go out and then come home and
then go out again?

A. No, he did not go out until after dinner.

Q. Did you not state over at the prison that he came in, found dinner was
not ready, went out, came in and went out?

A. I do not recollect saying so. I don't recollect what I said over at the
prison, for I was so confused and troubled I did not know what I said.

Q. Are you now certain that your statements are correct?

A. Yes, I am certain they are. . . .

Blake switched from John's alibi to William's alibi in his next question:

Q. Did you not state at the prison that it was about 3 o'clock when William
came in?

A. I do not recollect it.

Q. Are you now sure it was 4 o'clock.

A. Yes, I am sure it was.

The more she insisted on the time of John's and William's alibis, the surer
Blake was that the jury would assume she was lying to protect her sons
from the damaging admissions she had made in prison (*Trial*, 65–66).

A much more harmful statement was reportedly made by Mrs. Gordon
in the presence of Richard Knight before her arrest on the morning of
Tuesday, January 2:

Q. Did you make any statement to Gen. [General] Knight where John was
on the day of the murder?

A. I don't recollect anything about what I said.

Q. Do you recollect telling him that John came in about 5 o'clock, and said
Amasa Sprague was fixed?

A. I don't recollect saying so; don't know what I said. I was out of my mind
that day; was so agitated that I did not know what I was about.

Her agitation and confusion were understandable, for her new life in
America with her sons had suddenly collapsed with the arrest of John and
Nicholas the night before. Yet if she had actually told Richard Knight that
her son John came in about 5:00 P.M. the day of the murder and said
Amasa Sprague was "fixed," she had real reason to be agitated and "out of
her mind," since she had helped convict him on the spot (*Trial*, 67–68).

BROTHERLY LOVE

In the cross-examination, Mrs. Gordon was vague about Nicholas's gun:

A. I don't know much about it. There was a gun there soon after I came there.
Q. Did you ever see John with a gun?
A. I might have seen him, can't say. (*Trial*, 66)

Since testimony had already been given linking both Nicholas and John to the murder weapon, little that she could say about a gun would make much difference, but she did offer two explanations for any bloodlike stains on John's clothing taken in evidence by the prosecution. On Christmas Day, she said, John had come home with a turkey; she had wanted him to change his clothes because they were wet from his fall, "but he would not until he had killed the turkey; then he changed his pantaloons and put on dry" (*Trial*, 65). Moreover, she stated upon cross-examination that since John had worked at the Drybrook factory, she had had to boil his buff vest "to get the madder stains out." Madder, a bright red dye, was commonly used in printing calico cloth. Once fixed in the dyeing process with a solution of alumina, the color becomes fast. No forensic tests were undertaken by the prosecution to determine if the stain on John's shirt was caused by madder dye. But even more incomprehensible was that defense counsel had not done such a test on the shirt.

There followed a comedy of errors in which Mrs. Gordon insisted there were no "wet clothes" in the house from the Friday before the murder to the Tuesday following, when "wet clothes" were taken in evidence. What she meant was that she had not "wet" the clothes preparatory to cleaning them, whereas the prosecution meant the "wet" clothes taken in evidence, implying that John had stepped into the swamp after the murder. Of one thing she was certain: "Never saw such a coat [the coat found in the swamp] as that on either of my boys" (*Trial*, 67).

At this point Mrs. Gordon felt faint and was allowed to leave the courtroom. "She seemed very feeble and sickly," the court reporter, Edwin C. Larned, observed (*Trial*, 67). Larned, the transcriber of the trial testimony, was no mere journalist. He had graduated from Brown University in 1840 at the age of twenty, and by the time of the trial had been admitted to the Rhode Island bar. He later married the daughter of Albert C. Greene, former attorney general. His conservatism is evident in the preface to his original truncated version of trial testimony, in which he paid tribute to Amasa Sprague's high standing in the community and spoke of his being mourned not only by his family but especially by "the poor, who often shared his hospitality, and many of whom were dependent upon him for employment." His bias is evident in his attributing Sprague's opposition to Nicholas Gordon's liquor license to an unflinching advocacy of the temperance movement and in ascribing to Nicholas Gordon a hatred so strong and deep that "he sought revenge in the death of his victim" (*Full Report,* 3–4).[6]

Larned was called by the prosecution as a witness to rebut Mrs. Gordon in regard to the time her son John returned home on Sunday. Larned had been at the prison when she was brought in on Tuesday and had been asked to take notes on her testimony. His transcription of her statement in condensed form was read to the jury: "John was at home about 2 o'clock; he remained a little while. He said he would walk out and perhaps dinner would be ready. He came in, dinner was not ready and he walked out again; came in about 4 o'clock. He walked out on the road and came back about 7 o'clock" (*Trial,* 71).[7] There is no indication of any cross-examination by the defense of Larned's testimony; since Larned was also the transcriber of the trial record, it cannot be ascertained whether no cross-examination took place or whether he had simply left it out of the transcript.

The final defense witnesses were called to establish an alternative theory of the murder, that a stranger with a gun, not John or William Gordon, was the murderer. James Stratton, who lived on the Johnston side of the murder site, testified that on the afternoon of the murder he saw from the window of his house "a man coming round by the brow of the hill" on Rodney Dyer's land. He was a stout man who wore a dark frock coat and a black hat, and he carried a gun. In all he saw the stranger for an hour during which time he moved toward the bridge but did no hunting so that Stratton thought him "a lazy gunner" rather than a suspicious person. Francis M'Clocklin testified next that he saw the same man from the window of his house next door to Stratton's. He described the man as tall, taller and stouter than either John or William Gordon. He could not see whether the man had a gun, but fifteen minutes after he first sighted the stranger, he heard the loud report of a gunshot (*Trial,* 75).

Finally, John O'Brien, who was out hunting that afternoon, testified that when he reached the haystacks between Dyer's bridge and the footbridge, he saw a man standing by an oak tree near Dyer's bridge, but when O'Brien spotted him he drew back out of sight. All three witnesses had reported this information to either Rollin Mathewson or Richard Knight, and O'Brien had actually pointed out the track made by the man to both Mathewson and Knight (*Trial,* 75). Yet the authorities ignored their evidence in the pretrial investigations.

The closing statements by the defense and prosecution attorneys were noteworthy for their length, if not for their conciseness of legal argument, equaling in the transcription the prosecution and defense testimony combined. These "arguments," as they were called, had the purpose of summarizing for the jury the salient points of evidence and testimony for or against the prisoners, putting it all together from one perspective or the other, emphasizing the strong points and leaving out or moving rapidly over any weak parts in the case. As such, the arguments were repetitious of the testimony, but served the purpose of arranging in logical order what at times was disconnected testimony.

Thomas Carpenter naturally emphasized that the evidence against the defendants was "strictly circumstantial" and circumstantial evidence, he argued, is notoriously unreliable and misleading even though seemingly convincing. He focused on the weak point in the prosecution's conspiracy theory: John and William's motive to commit murder. Their brother Nicholas, a combative, undersized Irishman, had threatened the hefty, broad-shouldered, nearly six foot Amasa Sprague over the loss of a liquor license. To assume that Nicholas actually wanted to murder Amasa because of the quarrel would be false. Even more falacious would be to assume that the two brothers would do murder just because Nicholas lost his license. Only the prostitute Susan Field said so, and she couldn't tell John from William and William from John, even though she pretended she knew them well (*Trial,* 91).

The court, Carpenter said, only permitted the testimony on Nicholas's motivation to be heard by the jury "for what it was worth," the implication being of course that it was worthless as far as the defense counsel was concerned. At this point Chief Justice Durfee indignantly interrupted Carpenter's argument: "No, sir, no sir; we permitted it to pass to the jury for them to determine what influence it might have had upon the minds of the prisoners, in the relation they then were to him" (*Trial,* 92). It was now up to the jury to determine what influence Durfee's "correction" of

Carpenter's argument had on its collective mind concerning the issue of motivation and its corollary, the conspiracy theory.

Thomas Carpenter then turned next to a consideration of William Gordon's innocence based on his alibi; this was his strongest argument in the defense of the Gordons. "William Gordon was not and could not have been there [at the murder scene]. We have proved this to a moral certainty" (*Trial*, 96). But if the defense was to triumph, the case against John Gordon had to be destroyed. Carpenter chipped away at the circumstantial evidence against John. The tracks—there were two separate sets of tracks, not continuous; it was not proved John made either of them although his boots fit the one. But the boots were a standard size, ready-made: "Why, Mr. Ormsbee tells you that they put these very boots into *his* tracks, and they fitted exactly" (*Trial*, 98). The gun—the prosecution could not prove definitely it was Nicholas's gun, let alone that John used it. "The village has been ransacked, and everybody has been produced—from Elder Risley, the minister, to Ben Kit, the fool; aye, and lower than that, to Susan Field, the inmate of the house of Susan Parr," and no one has been able "to connect Nicholas S. Gordon directly with this gun [the murder weapon]" (*Trial*, 102). Unspoken, of course, was the fact that the defense team had not been able to produce the gun that Nicholas Gordon had supposedly purchased. They were not required to, but undoubtedly the gun would have made a tremendous difference and considerably strengthened the defense's case.

The coat found hidden in the swampy area near the murder scene was undoubtedly worn by the murderer, Carpenter admitted, but was it the same coat owned by Nicholas Gordon? Witness after witness, including his sister and his mother, testified for the defense that they had never known Nicholas to wear or own such a coat. Yet there was no getting around the fact that some prosecution witnesses had identified the coat or one similar to it as being owned or worn by Nicholas. Hardin Hudson, who testified that Nicholas wore the coat in question, was too easily dismissed as prejudiced against the defense, mistaken in his testimony rather than perjured. Susan Field's testimony was dismissed out of hand on account of her character, but not George Beverly's: "I felt some anxiety about his testimony," Thomas Carpenter admitted, "from his known honesty, intelligence and observing character" (*Trial*, 105). But Beverly had changed his testimony and admitted he was mistaken about the coat. He finally said he had seen Nicholas wear a velvet-collared coat, not the bloodstained coat worn by the murderer, which was similar in general appearance but had no velvet collar.

Were it not for the web of suspicion the prosecution had woven around John Gordon, the bruise on his face and his wet clothes would be trivial, even comic, according to the defense. He was, it would seem, a bit prone to falling down on Christmas day, being "a little worse for liquor," according to his sister. Apparently on his way home from Fenner's tavern, carrying a live turkey for the holiday dinner and taking the very same short cut that Amasa Sprague used on the day of his murder but from the opposite direction, John Gordon "fell by the side of the bridge in the swamp and liked to have killed himself" (*Trial*, 63). This was not the same bridge on which Amasa Sprague was murdered—that would have been too coincidental—but the one closer to home, at Hawkins' Hole. "A little worse for liquor," John fell there while coming over the swamp and "was reeking wet" when he got back with the turkey. Then or later that night he fell down in the road three miles from home, so drunk that he could not get up, and thus acquired the bruise on his face. At any rate, in the morning fall into the swamp he was sober enough to hold on to the turkey.

Carpenter continued his argument in a more serious vein, citing the fact that the authorities were so confident they had the guilty ones that any reddish or brownish stain on clothing found in the Gordon household was assumed to be blood, but no chemical test was made to prove the stain on the shirt sleeve was blood, not red madder dye or even the brownish stain of beer. Yet the *Providence Journal* reported as fact: "a shirt found in Gordon's house had a bloody stain on the sleeve corresponding with the hole in the coat. . . . On the vests were spots of blood, and one of the sheets on the bed was also marked with blood."[8]

Carpenter then attempted to attack the legality of Edwin Larned's being allowed to read his notes describing Mrs. Gordon's statements during her examination while in prison on Tuesday, January 2: "the minutes which a witness takes at the time are not evidence. His memory alone is to be depended upon legally, but not his notes" (*Trial*, 111). At this point, Chief Justice Durfee interrupted Carpenter for the second time to remonstrate with him:

> The Court understood the minutes read by the witness, who took them down, to be admitted in evidence, by both parties, no objections being made to them at the time. If the counsel for the prisoners did not intend

these should pass as evidence, they should have made their objections at
the time. (*Trial*, 111)

The fact that Carpenter failed to object at the proper time is one more
example of his unconscionable lack of an aggressive strategy for the
defense of John and William Gordon. It was also an anticlimax to his long
closing argument. He could only end with a plea to the jury to believe
Ellen Gordon's testimony during the trial, not the statements she made
when arrested.

Samuel Atwell, in his briefer closing argument for the defense, took up
where his associate had left off, defending the integrity of Mrs. Gordon's
testimony in giving her son John an alibi for the time of the murder. In
order to offset the common belief that a mother would perjure herself to
defend a son, he presented an emotional portrait of an old woman who
was at the point of death and who had therefore told the truth and
nothing but the truth. "You must say that that old woman, with one foot
already in the grave, and whose hairs are whitening for the winter of
death, must have deliberately perjured herself, or John Gordon is innocent of this crime" (*Trial*, 117). Ironically, Samuel Atwell would be dead
within six months, whereas the old woman would live to suffer the trou-
bles of her sons.

In the course of going over the evidence of the tracks, Atwell asked the
jury to consider the set of tracks coming to the murder site from the
opposite direction, from the Johnston side:

Now we find a man—an armed man on the Johnston side—coming toward the place of the murder, just before the time it must have been committed. John Gordon was not found there at the time of the murder.
William Gordon was not found there; but we find another man on the
Johnston side of the river, whose tracks correspond exactly with those on
the Cranston side. . . . That man is seen on Dyer's hill, at the brow of the
hill; he is seen jumping from tree to tree, keeping himself concealed; he
has a gun in his hands; he had a dark colored frock coat on. He is next
seen by the end of the wall leaning toward the ledge of rocks. A quarter of
an hour after, the report of a gun is heard, and this corresponds with the
time of Amasa Sprague's murder. (*Trial*, 119)

Atwell then complained that the prosecution had kept this information
from the defense until the very last weekend of the trial, when he "forced

them [the prosecution] into a discovery and explanation of them" (*Trial*, 119).

This petulance on Atwell's part allowed William Potter, the prosecution attorney, to break whatever effect this strong argument for an alternative murder theory had on the jury. Potter got Atwell into a debate on who informed whom about what and when, and the dramatic effect of the defense's theory was dissipated by the spectacle of lawyers arguing among themselves. This was to have been the climax of Atwell's closing argument, and his going over the familiar pieces of evidence—the coat, the gun—seemed anticlimactic.

Atwell then attacked the character of Ben Kit and Susan Field, but in so doing he inadvertently revealed his own prejudice against the Irish, shared in common by native white Americans, that they were unreliable witnesses to the truth. "I have shown you that it was to be expected that these witnesses [for the defense] should be Irishmen and Catholics . . . yet though we have produced Irishmen, we have not produced either a fool or a——. . ." Here he paused as he faced the jury, then continued, "I have liked to have used a naughty word—a *young lady*, the inmate of Miss Susan Parr's" (*Trial*, 123).

Atwell ended his argument with the statement that the murderer was "the man who made the tracks by Dyer's Bridge, rather than John Gordon." He reminded the jury that "if there is any doubt about it, if it might have been another man, and that hypothesis fits as well the circumstances proved, you cannot, and so I ask the Court to charge the jury—you cannot convict John Gordon" (*Trial*, 123). Thus the case for the defense ended with an alternative theory of who had killed Amasa Sprague: according to the defense theory, the killer was the man seen stalking Amasa with a gun shortly before the murder by several witnesses—the Strattons, M'Clocklin, and O'Brien. The investigators had never followed up on this evidence even though John O'Brien had told Richard Knight and Rollin Mathewson about the man and shown them the tracks. Richard Knight was a Sprague man and Rollin Mathewson was Amasa Sprague's nephew. The implication was there for the jury to ponder—the investigators, taking their cue from William Sprague, had so prejudged the case and believed the Gordons guilty that they had never pursued an alternative clue.

In his closing argument for the prosecution Attorney General Joseph Blake insisted that the prisoners had had "a fair and impartial trial." This was said specifically in response to Atwell's suggestion that the prosecution had tried to hold back an important piece of testimony favorable to the defense, namely the existence of another man with a gun near the murder scene around the time of the murder, as James Stratton and others had testified. The attorney general claimed that the prosecution had fully cooperated with the defense; that nothing had been kept back, and that the accusation of withholding Stratton's name from the defense counsel was "wholly unfounded" (*Trial*, 124). But Blake also meant "fair and impartial" in the general sense that the rules of law and evidence had been properly followed. The prosecution could afford to be high-minded about the court's rulings on points of law—the court had ruled in the prosecution's favor in almost every instance, even to the point of turning the proceedings for all practical purposes into a trial of Nicholas Gordon as well as of John and William.

Despite the fact that Rhode Island's leading newspaper, the *Providence Journal*, had announced only two days after the murder that the guilty persons, the Gordons, had been arrested, Blake insisted the public mind had not been prejudiced by pretrial publicity, pointing to the fact that only three or four prospective jurors (actually the number was six) had to be dismissed on the ground that they had already formed an opinion as to the guilt or innocence of the prisoners. Furthermore, the family and friends of Amasa Sprague, the attorney general maintained, were not unduly "interested" in the trial, and that they had "no thirst for the blood of the prisoners," only a justifiable "interest in the detection of the murderers." Nonetheless, the involvement of the family and friends of Amasa Sprague, indeed of nearly the whole community in Mr. Sprague's village, as it was called by one of the witnesses, made it questionable whether the Gordons could have had a "fair and impartial trial."

The saga of the bloodstained coat worn by the murderer and identified by some of the prosecution witnesses as the one owned by Nicholas Gordon is sufficient to illustrate how closely the Sprague family and friends were involved in the gathering and securing of evidence for the trial. The coat was found hidden in the swamp by David Lawton, a villager, on Tuesday morning, January 2. It was handed over to Theodore Quinn who was in the group of investigators headed by Walter Beattie, a thirty-year-old Scotsman who worked as a machine printer at the Sprague mill. Beattie examined the contents of the pockets. Quinn then handed the coat to Alexander Boyd, who took it to Amasa's house and gave it to

Rollin Mathewson, Sprague's nephew. Several others were present when Boyd handed the coat over. The coat was at first put under a sofa in the Sprague house but later carried upstairs and locked in a trunk. The key to the trunk was handed over to Byron Sprague, Amasa's nephew and the only son of his brother William. The trunk was eventually put into the possession of Amasa's daughter, Mary Anna, and was turned over to the sheriff, Roger W. Potter, by Walter Beattie before the grand jury sat to consider the indictment of the Gordons. Presumably at the same time Beattie delivered John Gordon's boots and another trunk of clothes kept in Amasa Sprague's milk-house.

How much all this investigative activity was motivated by a public-spirited desire to see justice done and how much by the fact the town council and the Sprague family had each put up a reward of $1,000 for information leading to the arrest and conviction of the murderers will never be known, but Susan Field came forward with her vital information about the coat and Nicholas Gordon's alleged motivation within twenty-four hours. Nor can it be known who first in the village reported that Nicholas Gordon had had "trouble" with Amasa Sprague over the liquor license six months earlier since just about everyone remembered the quarrel, but John and Nicholas Gordon were arrested on suspicion of murder, even before the coat and the gun had been found. From the moment of the arrest the investigation was focused on the Gordons, and clues that did not substantiate their guilt, such as the tracks in the snow leading in the opposite direction from the ones leading to Gordon's house, were never investigated. Given the careless methods of investigation, it is debatable whether the Gordons could have had "a fair and impartial trial" even if they had been Yankee to the core, rather than recent Irish immigrants.

Shrewdly, Attorney General Blake turned this seemingly amateur sleuthing by dozens of investigators into proof of guilt by suggesting that it added up to a *variety* of circumstances, all tending to prove the same thing, the guilt of the Gordons. The discovery of the various pieces of evidence by different people at various times proved there was no conspiracy against the defendants: "The case is greatly strengthened and confirmed, from the fact that so many witnesses have testified, of both sexes and of different ages, of different ranks in life, of different habits and pursuits, from different places, testifying to different facts, but all tending to the same point, and all concentrating upon the prisoners at the bar" (*Trial*, 128). Was it cousin Stephen Sprague who first found the splintered piece of gun with blood and hair on it? Well, then, it was Nathan Pratt who on Tuesday found the gun hidden in the swamp near the coat, and it was Gardner Luther, the next day, as he picked about in the snow "where Mr. Sprague's head lay," who found several small pieces of the gun lock. They were all pieces from the gun used to beat Sprague to death, the gun others testified as belonging to Nicholas Gordon and therefore available to his brother John.

In his closing argument Blake concentrated on the case against John Gordon. But first he had to establish that Nicholas Gordon was the motivating force behind the murder. Nicholas, according to Blake, was the sworn "enemy of the deceased," not only because of the loss of the liquor license, but also because Amasa Sprague had forbidden his workers to enter Nicholas's store, telling them that he would "employ no one who contributed to sustain it by going there, or buying anything from it." This created in Nicholas a motive "of deadly hate and revenge" to commit murder. He, thereupon, conspired with his two brothers to kill Amasa Sprague" (*Trial*, 131).

Blake's anti-Irish prejudices became explicit: William and John Gordon, he asserted, came to America in the summer of 1843 "with the idea which is common to many of their countrymen, that the laws here, in this free country, are less severe, and may be more easily evaded, than the laws of their own country—that they would be less restrained in their indulgencies; and less liable to punishment here, than under the strict police of their own country." Their strongest loyalty would be to the family, and to Nicholas Gordon as the head of the family: "the tie of kindred is to an Irishman almost an indissoluble bond" (*Trial*, 132). The clear implication for the jury was that John and William Gordon, being Irish, would do anything for their brother Nicholas, even murder for him.

Historically, there was an element of generalized truth in Blake's anti-Irish comments, enough at least to feed upon the fears and prejudices of the jury. The traditional rural Irish family was, indeed, "uncompromisingly patriarchal."[9] The majority of immigrants were from isolated communities in Ireland where they could be arbitrarily dispossessed of their property by an unjust legal system controlled by the English.[10]

When they immigrated to Providence, they continued to center their lives around the family and by extension to the Irish community banded together in ethnic neighborhoods close to the church, like the other ethnic Catholic immigrants who followed them to work in the textile mills, the French Canadians and the Italians. The church was the center of their lives outside the workplace, being a secular as well as a religious focus. The Hibernian Orphan Society was established in the late 1830s to help needy orphans; a temperance society was founded in 1840, and a parochial school, the first in the state, was begun in 1843. As mentioned earlier, two associations to foster repeal of the Act of Union joining England and Ireland were formed in 1841. Although the Irish in Providence had no newspaper of their own, they avidly read the *Boston Pilot,* especially for any news from Ireland about the repeal movement. The *Boston Pilot* was identified at the trial as the newspaper Nicholas Gordon subscribed to through Jeremiah Baggott, the Providence agent.[11]

While the French Canadians and the Italian Catholic immigrants also established their own societies and associations and lived in defined community neighborhoods in their time, the Irish immigrants were especially wary of the Yankees, and they of them, because the antagonism particularly felt by the Irish toward the English sometimes transferred itself to the New England Yankee. That a Yankee landlord might possibly fear retributive vengeance from an Irish immigrant was not entirely without foundation. An editorial that Nicholas Gordon might have read in the *Boston Pilot* (January 28, 1843) declared:

> It is horrible to encounter the monthly record of the outrages and the distress occasioned by the *law* and the *landlords* in Ireland. Not an arrival but brings an account of one or more murders in consequence of the operation of the Landlord and Tenant Law, and all who peruse the record of it, cannot but execrate a government which thus gives life to crime and immunity to cruelty. We know of no cause so potent in its influence, in staining with blood the hands of the peasantry of Ireland, as this same Landlord Law, and we cannot find it in our heart to denounce as a murderer, him who, when his passions are roused and driven to extremest want, turns upon the author of his wretchedness, and reeks [*sic*] his vengeance.

However, to infer, as Attorney General Blake did, from general social and cultural patterns an individual mystical bond of Celtic brotherhood among the Gordon brothers sworn to do murder was to invent fiction.

Blake returned to the circumstantial evidence: John Gordon allegedly was seen with the gun. His boots matched the tracks in the snow. The coat was Nicholas Gordon's, according to testimony, worn by his brother John and hidden by him in the swamp after the murder. And even if the coat did not belong to Nicholas and was worn by a confederate rather than by John at the time of the murder, "it belonged to an *Irishman*. The paper found in the pocket, is a piece of an Irish newspaper, and has an Irish direction in writing upon it" (*Trial*, 136; italics in the original). The clear implication of Blake's prejudicial statement was that an Irish vendetta against Sprague had been carried out and that if Nicholas Gordon didn't own the coat or his brother John wear it, it didn't matter, the murderer who wore the coat was an Irishman, a confederate in the conspiracy.

Moreover, Blake continued, if the coat was not Nicholas's, "where is the other old coat. . . . Why is it not produced? No such coat was found in Nicholas Gordon's house. What had become of it?" (*Trial*, 137). Similarly, according to sworn testimony, John Gordon was seen with a gun two days before the murder. If this was not the same gun as the murder weapon, as witnesses had testified, then "where is the gun that John Gordon then had? What has become of it? Why has it not been accounted for? . . . They [pointing to the prisoners] knew this gun had been found when they were first arrested. It was damaging evidence against them. It stared them in the face. What did they say about it?" They said nothing about it; yet when "the officers entered the house on Monday night and made particular search for a gun," none was found (*Trial*, 139–40).

The tracks leading to the Gordon house that John Gordon's boots fitted were brought up as linking the series of circumstances leading to John Gordon's guilt. The shirt found in the Gordon house with a reddish stain on the sleeve was part of the pattern of circumstantial evidence pointing to John Gordon's guilt: the stain on the sleeve corresponded to where there was a hole in the bloodstained coat. Was the stain on the shirt blood? It had not been tested because Blake "did not believe that a mere stain upon a piece of cloth was susceptible of a chemical analysis." Defense attorney Samuel Currey interrupted the attorney general to say that a chemical analysis could easily have been done. Blake taunted Currey with his own lack of preparation: "Why did you not have it done? Did you not dare to have the experiment tried?" (*Trial*, 144). By the logic of this topsy-turvy argument, the defense, not the state or county officers, had to provide the evidence if it proved the Gordons *not* guilty. The prisoners, according to Blake, "are bound to explain" the state of their clothing. John Gordon had to prove it was *not* Amasa Sprague's blood even though the prosecution had not proved it was. Blake turned to face John Gordon:

"The charge is upon your house—upon your family, upon YOU! John Gordon, where were you on that fatal hour? Free yourself from the damning evidence of your guilt" (*Trial*, 146). Blake explicitly insisted that in cases such as this one in which the accused had no alibi (he dismissed Mrs. Gordon's testimony as contradictory and prejudiced), "the burden of proof . . . is upon the prisoners, and it must be fully made out" (*Trial*, 150).

Although the defense had produced witnesses who provided an alibi for William Gordon, the attorney general clung to his case against William by distorting the testimony of his own witnesses. He argued that William could have been the short man seen by Barker and Spencer the first time if they were mistaken about the time, that it was 1:00 P.M. rather than 2:00 P.M. as they testified. From 10:00 A.M. to 1:30 P.M. William's movements were "wholly unaccounted for," except for the testimony of Michael O'Brien, an unreliable witness from the prosecution's point of view. William could easily have gone back to Cranston in time to be the short man seen by Barker and Spencer, and then have run back to Providence in time to be seen at Baggott's house at 1:30 P.M. True, he was seen by Michael Holohan at mass in Providence which began at 10:00 A.M., but Michael "does not tell when or how long" William was in church (*Trial*, 148–49). The weakness of Blake's argument was patently obvious. The fact that he used it at all suggests how desperate he was to prevent his case against William Gordon from collapsing completely.

Seeing that the jurors were consulting their notes on the testimony of Barker and Spencer, Blake then insisted that if the jury were satisfied William was not the short man seen by Barker and Spencer the first time, then the two men "were in all probabilities confederates in the conspiracy." Furthermore, the defense still had to prove William was not the short man seen by Barker and Spencer the second time shortly after the murder (*Trial*, 150).

But according to the testimony of Joseph Cole, William Gordon could not have arrived back in Cranston in time to be the short man without a coat seen by Barker and Spencer the second time, shortly after the murder. Blake proceeded to attack Cole's credibility as a witness: "his appearance on the stand was very unfavorable," and his testimony was contradicted in particulars by Richard Knight. "So much," Blake said derisively, "for Mr. Joseph Cole" (*Trial*, 151). In other words, if the jurors believe the careful, considered testimony of witnesses like Barker and Spencer, they will find William guilty as well as John Gordon. If they believe witnesses like Michael O'Brien and Joseph Cole, they will find William innocent and John Gordon guilty.

Under Dorr's People's Constitution the jury in all criminal cases would have been sole judge "both of the case and of the facts." But under the new constitution that went into effect in 1843, the judges of the supreme court were given the power to "instruct the jury on the law" in all trials. Thus in his charge to the jury, Chief Justice Durfee instructed the jurors at great length about the law as he saw it. He paid tribute to the ideal of justice that every man is innocent until he is proved guilty and that the jurors must be satisfied beyond a reasonable doubt of the guilt of each of the accused as separate individuals before finding either one or both guilty. Having said that, he backed the contention of the prosecution that circumstantial evidence is equally conclusive with positive testimony where it satisfies the mind, particularly when "the testimony of each witness constitutes a link in the chain," as in this case.

On the question of motive for the crime, Durfee explained to the jury that he had permitted "evidence of hostile feeling . . . expressed by Nicholas S. Gordon" so that "you may draw such inference from it as you think the facts shall justify. . . . You are to give it such weight as you think proper; you are to determine for yourselves what effect his declared enmity would have upon the minds of the prisoners situated as they then were in relation to Nicholas S. Gordon" (*Trial*, 78). This was a careful summation of the ruling he had made in favor of the prosecution.

When it came to instructing the jury on the conflicting and contradictory testimony concerning William Gordon's alibi, Chief Justice Durfee clearly overstepped the bounds of judicial fairness and impartiality. He had been careful to point out that where conflicting testimony is of "equal force," the defendant must be acquitted "on the ground that he is presumed innocent until he is proved guilty." But he went on: "You will understand me here as speaking in relation to the testimony of Barker and Spencer on the one hand, and of the countrymen of William Gordon on the other" (*Trial*, 78). He denied he was weighing the credibility of the witnesses. Yet he continued:

When a witness testifies to fact, not inconsistent with the undoubted evidence in the case, and his character for truth is in no way impeached, and his testimony is not brought in question or doubt by the cross-examination, or by his previous declarations, or otherwise, he is entitled to full credit as a witness, who ever he may be. (*Trial,* 79)

In the context of the anti-Irish and anti-Catholic atmosphere that existed in Rhode Island at the time and in the specific context of the anti-Irish bias of the prosecution, the jury would have understood the distinction Durfee was making between the Yankees, Barker and Spencer, and Irish witnesses such as Michael O'Brien and Joseph Cole. Attorney General Blake had made it clear in his closing argument what he thought of the relative merits of the Barker-Spencer and the O'Brien-Cole testimony. With closing statements of the attorney general fresh in their minds, the members of the jury could not help concluding that Chief Justice Durfee's "who ever" was Barker-Spencer.

Durfee then took up the testimony of Mrs. Gordon. In estimating her credibility as a witness, he admonished the jury: "You will necessarily consider the relation in which she stands to the accused; her manner of testifying here; the consistency of her story with undoubted facts in the case; her declarations to Mr. Knight . . . and her evidence given before the magistrate, and read here by the witness who took it down in writing" (*Trial,* 79). From a legal perspective it was a fair summary of the status of the mother's testimony, but by implication Chief Justice Durfee made clear what he thought her testimony was worth. No reference was made to her fear and confusion when she made the damaging statements to Richard Knight and to the examining magistrate.

Referring to the defense's alternative theory that a stranger, not John Gordon, was the murderer, Chief Justice Durfee charged the jury that "it will be your duty to enquire whether it be or be not consistent with the undoubted facts and evidence" (*Trial,* 79–80). Durfee then proceeded to demonstrate how much he considered had to be assumed for the defense's theory to fit the prosecution's case of circumstantial evidence, despite the fact that the prosecution's evidence about the gun and the coat was contradicted by testimony from defense witnesses:

> Did this unknown man wear boots of like size with those which John Gordon claimed as his? Did he, instead of returning by the route on which he came, shape his course towards Gordon's house? Did he happen to have the gun that was seen in the possession of John Gordon but a few days before, or one so like it, that the witness cannot see the slightest difference? Did he have the pistol here shown? Did he happen to have the coat with

the short hair upon it; and a coat so very like the one in the possession of
the Gordons that it may not be easily distinguished from it? Did he direct
his footsteps to Gordon's back door, and there stop without entering the
house? (*Trial*, 80)

Only if the answer was yes to all these questions could the hypothesis be
established as a true alternative to the supposition of John Gordon's guilt:
"But you are not at liberty to *suppose* these facts to be so. They must be
proved, or they must be fairly inferred from the evidence in the case"
(*Trial*, 80, italics in the original).

In his final charge to the jury, Chief Justice Durfee returned to the issue
of the credibility of witnesses when weighing contradictory testimony. His
bias was evident in his instructions: when "witnesses be of equal credibility" and contradict each other, "no legitimate inference can be drawn
from their testimony"; but when "one has the better opportunity to know
the facts than the other, that one must be believed in preference to the
other," for "questions of identity are often questions of belief" (*Trial*, 80).
In the context of the trial as a whole and in the specific context of his
summation, Durfee could only mean whom do you believe—native-born
Yankees or immigrant Irishmen; the citizens of the community and the
authorities or the fellow countrymen and relatives of the accused? Similarly, Durfee instructed the jury that "questions of time are also questions
of belief, where a person has no artificial means of measuring it, and in all
these questions, we must be governed mainly by the belief and opinions of
those who are the best able to judge, or have the best opportunity of
judging, and their judgment may be rectified and reconciled by these
undoubted facts in the case which make up the great body of the evidence" (*Trial*, 80).

Chief Justice Durfee ended his remarks by reasserting the principle of
reasonable doubt, that a guilty verdict required the jury to be satisfied
beyond a reasonable doubt, but if they were not fully satisfied the verdict
must be acquittal. He then recessed the court at 6:30 P.M., and the jury
retired to consider its verdict.

The jury took only an hour and fifteen minutes to come to a verdict:

Clerk. Have you agreed on a verdict?
Foreman. We have.
Clerk. Gentlemen of the jury, who shall speak for you?
Jurors. Our foreman.

> Clerk. Prisoners, look on the jurors—jurors, look on the prisoner; what
> say, Mr. Foreman, is John Gordon guilty or not guilty?
> Foreman. GUILTY.
> Clerk. Gentlemen of the jury, as your foreman hath said, so do you all say?
> Jurors. We do.
> Clerk. Prisoner, look on the jurors—jurors, look on the prisoner; what say
> you, Mr. Foreman, do you find William Gordon guilty, or not guilty?
> Foreman. NOT GUILTY. (*Trial*, 80–81)

John Gordon, the full implication of his conviction breaking his out-ward calm, then turned to his brother and said, "It is you, William, that have hung me" (*Full Report*, 60). What William had done to cause John to accuse him of betrayal was not revealed until nine months later.

The proceedings in the court continued, the form of justice being followed to the letter of the law and tradition: the verdicts were recorded by the clerk, and then read by him to the jury:

> Clerk. Gentlemen of the jury, hearken to your verdict, as the Court have
> recorded it. We find John Gordon guilty of the felony whereof he stands
> indicted. We find William Gordon not guilty. Is that your verdict, gentle-
> men?
> Jurors. It is. (*Trial*, 81)

As the tension in the courtroom broke, William, now a free man, was congratulated by his friends and lawyers. John, who throughout the trial had sat next to his brother, now sat alone. As a reporter for the Providence *Transcript* observed, "his dejected and desolate look and condition are almost sufficient to draw tears from the eyes of Justice herself."[12]

The Providence correspondent of the *Boston Pilot* reflected the more general indignation of the Irish community at the prejudice against the Gordons and the Irish revealed during the trial:

> I am sorry to have it to say there never was a trial in this country where a
> worse feeling of prejudice has been shown, than has been exhibited in the
> present one; it has lasted nine days, and the Government spared neither
> time nor money to scratch up every thing they could get in the shape of
> evidence; they called up a common idiot that travels round the streets, that
> might know nothing of humanity more than the most savage animal that
> roams the forest, named Ben Waterman, and a woman who is well known
> to both Judge and Jury and all concerned, to be a common prostitute,

named Susan Field; she told the counsel on her cross-examination, that
she could answer him quicker than he could question her; and yet her testimony was more handled with reliance than all the others of fifty or sixty
witnesses for the State. She testified that she heard Nicholas Gordon, in
the presence of John Gordon, swear that he would take the life of Amasa
Sprague, to be revenged of him for stopping his License, and when their
counsel asked her could she identify William and John separately by their
names, she answered yes, and turned round on her oath and said that
[pointing to them separately] is William, and that is John, which is just
the reverse; and still her testimony was taken, as I said before, with great
reliance.[13]

The "tears of Justice," implied the correspondent for the *Boston Pilot,*
were ones of outrage, not sadness, in the Providence Irish community.

CHAPTER FIVE

Nicholas Gordon's
First Trial

The post-trial legal maneuvering between the two sets of lawyers began almost immediately. Thursday, the day following the verdict, the defense attorneys moved that John Gordon's sentencing be deferred until after the trial of his brother Nicholas. In support of the motion, it was cited that Samuel Atwell was seriously ill and unable to participate for the present. Second, and more important to the defendant, the defense argued that facts might come out that would show John Gordon was innocent. William Potter, speaking for the prosecution, opposed the motion on the grounds that the guilty verdict was "a true verdict" after a full and impartial trial. Nicholas Gordon, he asserted, had had ample time to explain the facts both before and during the trial, but he had remained silent; if he knew any fact that would save his brother's life, then was the time to have revealed it. "Public justice and the welfare of the community," Potter argued, require "that the crime, the conviction and the execution should be seen together" as a continuum in which "the penalty of the law followed quick upon its violation" (*Trial*, 82–84). In short, hang him without delay as a deterrent to other criminals and as an example to all.

The court saw no reason to postpone sentencing, but said it would entertain a petition for a new trial if the counsel for the prisoners wished to do so the following morning. The next morning, Friday, April 19, 1844, John Gordon was brought before the court and Attorney General Blake moved "that the sentence of death . . . be pronounced upon him" (*Trial*, 83). It was then that John Knowles for the defense presented a petition for a new trial and moved that the hearing on the petition be postponed until the October term of the Court because Samuel Atwell, principal counsel for the Gordons, was absent, severely ill. The attorney general opposed any delay, arguing that the petition should be "tried" then and there, or no later than the next day. At the very least he wanted a hearing during the current term. The court, mindful of the impending Dorr trial, insisted that there was no time before the end of term in July to consider the motions, the calendar being full. The petition for a new trial for John Gordon was moved on the grounds that the prosecution had presented evidence of Nicholas Gordon's hostility to Amasa Sprague without first proving a conspiracy, and that notes of Ellen Gordon's testimony before the examining magistrate were allowed to be read even though the witness stated that he had no recollection of the testimony itself. The court ruled that a hearing on the petition would take place the afternoon of the first day of the next term. The defense got part of what it wanted, postponement of sentencing, since the hearing on the petition would have to precede setting a date for execution. But the prosecution also got part of what it wanted—a commitment that a hearing would take place *before* Nicholas Gordon's trial in October.[1]

On May 1, 1844, in the emotional aftermath of the Gordon trial, one of the two sons of Amasa Sprague was assaulted and severely beaten. In the newspaper report of the attack, the assailant was identified as an Irishman who had acted "without the slightest provocation being offered by the injured party." No clue to the assailant's identity was found, but the boy was reported to be "in a very critical situation, from the injuries received."[2] The following day further details were revealed: "There is no doubt that the villian [*sic*] contemplated taking the life of the young man, as he first made sure of his identity and then attacked him with a club which he had concealed about his person." Amasa Sprague's son had recovered from the beating sufficiently to give details and was reported well, but the newspaper account no longer referred to the attacker as an Irishman.[3]

In addition to the emotions aroused in the Providence Irish community by the guilty verdict against John Gordon, the political atmosphere in Rhode Island was tense and potentially violent in the weeks that followed the Gordon trial. Many of the same Irish supporters of the Gordons were also supporters of Thomas Dorr, whose trial on the charge of treason began on April 26, 1844, just eight days after the John Gordon verdict.

The venue for Dorr's trial was changed by the court from Providence to Newport at the request of the prosecution, a patently political decision that removed Dorr from the jurisdiction of potentially more sympathetic jurors to a pool of jurors in Newport County that were anti-Dorrite almost

Thomas Wilson Dorr (1805–1854), 1845

to a man. Only 3 of the 118 jurors examined were Dorrites, and all 12 of the jurors finally selected "were to a man Algerines and Whigs."[4] Dorr, himself a lawyer, had originally opposed the change of venue as unconstitutional but he waived the issue of jurisdiction in order to get the trial over with; unfortunately, it was a decision that assured his conviction. As it was, 83 of the 118 jurors were dismissed for having already formed an opinion as to Dorr's guilt or innocence.

From the beginning the bias of two of the justices was evident. In the selection process for the jury, Chief Justice Durfee and Justice Levi Haile strongly favored the prosecution's proposal to ask each juror two loaded political questions in order to weed out any possible closet Dorrites from the jury: *"Did you vote for the said Thomas Wilson Dorr, for governor, at the election on the 18th of April, 1842?"* and *"Have you formed the opinion, or do you believe that the said Thomas W. Dorr was the Governor of the State, or authorized to exercise the duties of Governor, anytime between the 16th day of May, 1842, and the 28th day of June, 1842?"* But the court was evenly divided and the questions were not asked.[5]

Dorr pleaded innocent to the charge of treason against the state of Rhode Island. In fact, his main defense was that no such crime existed, because "treason is an offense against the United States only and cannot be committed against an individual State."[6] Realizing he had made a mistake in waiving change of venue, Dorr cited English law, using the defense that he must be tried in the county (Providence) in which the indictment was made, but the court ruled the change was proper.

Samuel Atwell, the Gordon brothers' attorney, was supposed to be Dorr's principal legal counsel, but he was still seriously ill. For the most part, Dorr conducted his own case; Atwell provided a written final argument and appeared only after the verdict to make a final plea against sentencing. Dorr was assisted by George Turner of Newport and Walter S. Burges of Providence. Burges was Dorr's mentor, close friend and ally in the suffrage movement; he was also from an old Providence family and was married to the daughter of U.S. Senator George R. Burrill. An early proponent of equal rights, Burrill argued in 1797 for a new constitution created and enacted by the people themselves, not the state legislature.[7] Turner, a Newport Democrat and a political ally of Dorr, argued the constitutional issue at great length during the trial. But Dorr himself dominated the trial as he argued that "treason, which is defined by the [U.S.] Constitution, and punished by the laws, of the United States, excluded all separate State treason, even if the exclusion be not in express terms."[8]

The prosecution was again led by Attorney General Joseph Blake, assisted by Alfred Bosworth of Warren, Rhode Island. Bosworth, a graduate of Brown University, came to the trial with excellent credentials from Blake's point of view, for he had served as a member of a special board of commissioners appointed by the military government to examine the 250 Dorrites arrested under martial law after the defeat of Dorr in June 1842.

The zealousness of the government in prosecuting the Dorrites was "censurable," according to Arthur May Mowry, a conservative historian of the Dorr war, "not only for the exceedingly large number of arrests, but for the indiscriminate character of the arrests, the methods of making them, and the treatment of their families, thus suddenly deprived of bread winners."[9] The most celebrated case of arrest under the martial law involved a Warren man, Martin Luther, a shoemaker, who was indicted for serving as moderator and receiving votes in a town meeting held in Warren under the People's Constitution. The case eventually went to the U.S. Supreme Court (Luther vs. Borden) in 1848. The main issue was the same one that dominated Dorr's trial: Had the people of Rhode Island a right to adopt a state constitution for themselves, establishing a government by the people? In 1849 the U.S. Supreme Court under Chief Justice Taney upheld the Rhode Island supreme court's position that it "could not traverse judicially the authority of the government under which it acted." The U.S. Supreme Court also ruled that it had no power to determine whether a state government had been lawfully established.[10]

Dorr's main objective in returning from exile to stand trial was to use the trial as a forum for his belief that the state was constituted by the will of the people. His principal defense was that he had acted upon the authority invested in him by the people. While Dorr's doctrine of popular sovereignty provided the theoretical framework for his later actions, he insisted in his defense that the act of establishing a people's government with himself as governor was not treasonable but a legally justified action sanctioned by the adoption of a valid constitution and ratified by a vote of the majority of the people. Having been duly elected governor on April 18, 1842, by the Dorrites, he considered he was duty bound to uphold and defend the people's constitution against any opposition. The opposition considered the very act of establishing a rival government an act of treason against the state.

Not all of the testimony was on such a high plane of constitutional theory. Dorr also wanted to answer charges concerning damages done to private property by his followers for which he, as their leader, felt personally responsible: some boards had been stolen and burnt, a horse had been borrowed, and a cow had been killed. The horse, he assured the jury, had been returned, and restitution had been made for the cow. Nothing was reported about compensation for the boards.[11]

At the end of his closing argument, however, Dorr returned to the theme of the sovereignty of the people. He affirmed his confidence that ultimately his beliefs would prevail: "I commit my case in your hands with the confidence in the final verdict of my country."[12] His confidence was in the jury of national political opinion, not in the jury of the twelve anti-Dorrites facing him.

The case for the prosecution was determined by the parameters of the popular sovereignty/state sovereignty issues at the center of the Dorr Rebellion: Attorney Bosworth argued that states are sovereign in every matter not specifically yielded to the federal government and that, as a sovereign entity, the state is distinct from the people and has the right to protect itself against acts of treason. Attorney General Blake did not need to argue the point because Chief Justice Durfee made it clear in his instructions to the jury that the court was unanimous in its opinion that "the sovereign authority of the State is such that treason can be committed against it."[13]

On May 7, 1844, the jury found Dorr guilty of treason. As one juror afterwards explained, "The Court made everything plain for us." All appeals were dismissed, and Chief Justice Durfee sentenced Dorr to prison "for the term of his natural life, and there kept at hard labor in separate confinement."[14]

In his statement to the court before being sentenced, Dorr pointed out that three of the jurors had expressed extreme hostility against him personally before being empanelled and that after the verdict the same three jurors had expressed a wish that Dorr be executed. However, the court had refused to allow the defense's attempt to prove this prejudice against him. The verdict was imposed, he claimed, in the spirit of political revenge rather than legal justice. In the end, Dorr, having charged the court with bias, appealed to the judgment of the people.[15]

The bias of the court and the jury was so extreme in this case that it was a foregone conclusion Dorr would be found guilty, but the severity of the sentence was nonetheless a shock. The editor of the *Boston Pilot* felt compelled to comment to a Fourth of July audience of the Providence Catholic community on "the recent odious sentence of Mr. Dorr. Although the *Pilot* has no connection with politics, its editor, as an individual and an advocate of liberty, could not and would not conceal his detestation of what he considered a great and grievous injustice."[16]

The sentence of solitary confinement was strictly enforced because of the fear that Dorr might stir up political rebellion in the state again. Solitary confinement, adopted in Rhode Island in 1838 and based on the harsh system used in Pennsylvania, had been made possible by the construction of the new state prison with forty cells, replacing the old Providence County Jail in which only eight cells had accommodated as many as thirty or more prisoners. The prisoner was kept in his cell even while doing manual labor and saw only his keeper, talking to him only when permitted. Consequently, six of the thirty-seven prisoners in the new prison "became hopelessly insane. As a result of recurring cases in insanity, mandatory solitary confinement was abandoned in 1843."[17] Dorr's sentence was especially severe. He was forbidden to write; he was forbidden visits except by his lawyer, and even his parents were often refused access; he was forbidden exercise in the prison corridors, and he was even refused requests for books other than religious ones. The effect of these restrictions was to make him seem a martyr, though no such purpose had been in the minds of his prosecutors or his jailers.[18]

In the meantime both John and Nicholas Gordon languished in prison, John waiting for a hearing on the appeal for a new trial, and Nicholas waiting for his trial to begin. They were kept isolated from each other and from the rest of the family. It was not until October 9, nearly six months after the trial, that the supreme court heard arguments on the motion for a new trial for John Gordon. But then justice was swift. By 4:00 P.M. that same day, in time for the *Transcript* to publish an extra, the hearing was over, the petition for a new trial had been denied, and John Gordon sentenced to death by hanging on February 14, 1845, between the hours of 10:00 A.M. and 12 noon. Chief Justice Durfee emphasized the brutality of the murder and the fairness and impartiality of the trial. At the end he turned to the prisoner and urged him to make his peace with God.

When asked why the sentence of death should not be passed upon him, John Gordon stated,

> Gentlemen, these may be my last words, I therefore here declare, that I never had hand, act or part in the murder of Mr. Sprague. I never had hand, act or part in the murder of any man, woman or child. I further declare, that I never knew that gentleman. My prosecutors have wickedly and maliciously sworn away my life, and it is always more easy to do to a stranger, than towards one who is well known. I have no more than this to say.[19]

It was the first, but not the last, word of John Gordon in his own defense. And it was not the confession of guilt and remorse for his actions that the court and the prosecution wanted to hear.

The following Monday, October 13, the trial of Nicholas Gordon began. The justices hearing the case were the same, as were the prosecutors trying the case, Attorney General Blake and William Potter, but the defense counsel had changed. Samuel Atwell was dying and Thomas Carpenter had been replaced by Samuel Currey as the principal counsel for the defense. A conservative in politics and religion (a Law and Order anti-Dorrite and a Calvinistic Baptist), Currey gave the defense a very different political profile. Like Nicholas Gordon, Currey was a naturalized citizen (from Canada), but unlike Gordon, he was very much part of the establishment in Rhode Island political and legal circles.[20] Perhaps because he was as conservative as any of the prosecution lawyers, he saw his role in the courtroom contest more in legal terms than did the politically liberal team of Atwell, Carpenter, and Knowles. Certainly he conducted a more aggressive and effective defense than had the others in the John and William Gordon trial.

To achieve a bolder defense Currey chose as his associate an aggressive trial lawyer from Boston, Jonathan B. Rogers. Some of the money to pay for the defense came from the Irish community of Boston as well as from the one in Providence, and the choice of Rogers may have been a concession to them. In effect, it broke the cozy circle of Rhode Island lawyers who dominated the previous trial. Charles Hart, a young Providence lawyer in Currey's office who, like Currey, had graduated from Brown University, completed the defense team.[21]

The jury was selected from a panel of forty-eight. Twenty-two of them were dismissed from duty as having already formed or expressed an opinion as to the guilt or innocence of the defendant. Three further possible jurors were dismissed because they had conscientious scruples against finding a man guilty of a crime that the law punishes with death. And finally eleven more, the maximum, were peremptorily challenged by the defense counsel, leaving the twelve men remaining to form the jury. Jonathan B. Sisson, a gardener living in Providence, was chosen foreman.[22]

On the surface, the trial of Nicholas Gordon seemed merely a replay of the William and John Gordon trial. In fact, much of the testimony was the same, not only because the details of the murder and the evidence were reintroduced in this trial but also because Nicholas Gordon had been tried in absentia with his two brothers during the first trial. Since the testimony was repetitious, the Providence *Transcript* (which had published a truncated, biased version of the John and William trial, leaving out all cross-examination of prosecution witnesses by the defense and all testimony by defense witnesses) now published only "any new matters" it deemed worthy. Unlike the earlier trial in which the court had requested no newspaper coverage during the proceedings, the press was allowed to report the court proceedings each day.

The specific charge in the indictment against Nicholas Gordon was that "he of his malice aforethought stirred up, moved, hired, counselled, abetted and procured John Gordon, William Gordon, and in one or more counts another person . . . unknown to perpetrate this crime."[23] What lay behind this seemingly straightforward repetition of the charge that Nicholas Gordon was an accessory before the fact to murder was a complicated legal maneuver by the prosecution to read into the record the fact that John Gordon had been convicted of committing the murder. "That record," Chief Justice Durfee stated in his charge to the jury, "is evidence as to him conclusive of his guilt . . . which is not to be controverted—that which no evidence can overcome."[24] Since John's conviction was prima facie evidence against Nicholas, the defense counsel would have to prove John Gordon innocent beyond a reasonable doubt before John's innocence could be used as evidence to help prove Nicholas innocent. The defense counsel argued that the record of John Gordon's guilty verdict was evidence only that he had been put on trial and convicted and nothing more. In other words, the defense was asking to be entitled to raise the issue of John Gordon's guilt "as a new and original question, with every legal presumption in favor of innocence against it."[25] The court ruled against the defense and in favor of the prosecution.

Samuel Currey also took exception to Chief Justice Durfee's instructions to the jury concerning the conviction of John Gordon as prima facie evidence against Nicholas Gordon. He insisted the court should instruct the jury that John Gordon's conviction was evidence only of the fact itself for the purpose of bringing Nicholas Gordon to trial as an accessory, but that it was no further evidence as to the *cause* (Nicholas Gordon's incitement of John to do murder). Furthermore, Currey argued, the court should charge the jury that it is "the exclusive province of the Jury to decide all questions of law as well as of fact."[26] This was a bold and startling attempt to get around the constant, unfavorable rulings of the court: bold in that it challenged the powers granted the supreme court by the new state constitution; startling in that Currey, a conservative, would argue in favor of a Dorrite understanding of the powers of a jury. For if Dorr's People's Constitution had prevailed, the court would have to rule as Currey proposed; the People's Constitution specified that "in all criminal cases the jury shall judge both of the law and of the facts."[27] Durfee, however, after consulting with the other justices, ruled that the court could not charge the jury other than it did.

The justices assumed a dual role throughout all three Gordon trials; they acted both as presiding trial judges and as a supreme court of final appeal, having the power to decide points of law without further appeal except to themselves. Under the new state constitution, the judges of the supreme court were charged with instructing the jury in the law. Chancery powers were the exclusive province of the supreme court, acting as a court of final appeal. When the chief justice conferred with his colleagues, he was thus consulting with them as a chancery court modeled on English law, as well as trial judges in a criminal case. Any question of law raised by the defense or the prosecution counsel was decided by the justices and their decision was final. A conspiracy trial for murder was so rare in Rhode Island that the present court mainly set its own precedents. Under the state constitution of 1843, they were right to rule as they did, but they very rarely gave the benefit of the doubt to the accused in any of the three trials. The prevailing legal and social climate strongly favored the political conservatism of the prosecution, not the accused.

The emphasis in the testimony was again on Nicholas Gordon's motivation and on his possession of a gun, a pistol, and an old coat. The prosecution through its witnesses again provided Nicholas with an alibi for the time of the murder, in order to prove him an accessory *before* the fact, instigating others to commit the crime, and not "an accessory *at* the fact" of committing the murder. The prosecution knew Nicholas had an alibi, and if they had indicted him as one who was present aiding and abetting in the commission of the crime, Nicholas, like his brother William, would have had to be found not guilty. It suited the prosecution's theory of the case that Nicholas *conspired* to get others to actually commit the murder. This fit in with the explanation of his absence from Cranston on the day of the murder, for he would naturally, having planned ahead of time, provided himself with an alibi. The fact that Sunday was the day he would usually be in Providence rather than Cranston to attend church and visit was used as evidence against him whereas William's alibi gained him acquittal.

The first day of testimony contained no surprises, being a repetition of factual evidence relating to the discovery of the body and the wounds. We learn for the first time that John Gordon was a slightly built man, under-sized, weighing about 130 pounds. The implication the defense counsel wished to leave was that John could not have overcome Amasa Sprague who was described by Dr. Lewis Miller on cross-examination as "a large athletic man," but then the prosecution had never suggested that John Gordon acted alone. Besides, Dr. Miller testified, the gunshot wound on Sprague's right arm would have disabled him. In the end all it proved was that John Gordon could not have been the tall man seen by Barker and Spencer, but then the prosecution was unconcerned, for he was already convicted. We also learn for the first time that the important "Irish direction" written upon the piece of Irish newspaper in the pocket of the coat found near the murder scene was "Tiperary" [*sic*].[28] Not until the second day, Wednesday, October 16, was significant new testimony revealed about the gun by prosecution witnesses. Deputy Sheriff Jabez Potter, accompanied by Daniel Chafee, had searched Nicholas's house and found no gun. Potter had then gone to the prison and interviewed Nicholas Gordon:

> I asked Nicholas how many guns he had, he said he had one, I asked him where the gun was. He said it was in the store. I told him we searched the store the night before, when he was present, and found no gun. He said, I think, the dog threw it down a day or two before, and he then placed it behind a barrel or more of oil.

Dr. Cleaveland, the jailer, then testified:

> I went to the cell with Mr. Potter and heard what Nicholas said to him about the gun. Afterwards I was in his cell, he seemed anxious about his gun and requested me to go into his shop and look for it, this was Tuesday in the forenoon, soon after Mr. Potter and myself had been with the prisoner. He gave me the key, I went to the store and found that the door had been forced between the house and shop, several men were in the shop. Don't know whether they had found a gun or not, I found none.[29]

Two or three of the persons who had broken into the shop were officers, but others were obviously villagers searching for "evidence."

During this conversation with Dr. Cleaveland, Nicholas revealed that he had at one time or another owned several guns. The only gun he now owned had been purchased from Tillinghast Almy in September 1843, three months before the murder. That was the gun which should have been in the store. Nicholas was so convinced that the gun would be found hidden in the store behind the oil cans that he was anxious to have them look again. The gun had to be there. But it was never found anywhere in the store or in the house by the officers, and that was important circumstantial evidence against him and his brothers.

Testimony about the pistol found at the murder scene was never conclusive because the pistol was not definitely identified as belonging to Nicholas either in the previous trial or in the present trial. During the first trial Attorney General Blake sought to link the pistol to Nicholas, claiming that "the powder found in the pistol exactly corresponded with the powder found in the coat" (*Trial*, 140). The forensic proof rested on the testimony of John M. Shaw, a constable, who had stated that the powder found in the pistol and in a box in the coat "appears to be the same" as the gunpowder found in the Gordon store and in a paper twist discovered in a pocket of one of the vests taken from Gordon's home. In Nicholas's trial, however, Shaw backed away from the positive statement he had made in the earlier trial and admitted he could perceive a difference between the powder found at the murder scene and the powder found in Gordon's store and house. The prosecution's expert witness, Duty Green, a Providence apothecary who had thirty years' experience dealing in gunpowder, also testified that the powder was different in the two instances. He had come to the conclusion by rubbing first one and then the other, finding the latter to be softer, and then he tasted first one and then the other, finding the latter to be sharper and stronger in taste.[30] To retrieve the situation as best he could, Blake elicited testimony that Amasa Sprague had owned a Colt revolver quite unlike the single shot pistol found near his dead body. He had, moreover, never carried it "but once; when he went to Chepachet" in June 1842. Chepachet was Thomas Dorr's stronghold, and also Dorr's last stand. Going *to* Chepachet meant you were a "Law and Order" man ready to do battle with the Dorrites.

There were slight differences in testimony between the two trials even when the same ground was covered by the same witness. For example, in the first trial Abner Sprague, Jr., was certain that the gun he had seen John Gordon carry two days before the murder was the murder weapon—"I have no doubt of it at all," he had testified. In Nicholas's trial, his testimony upon cross-examination was much more uncertain: the murder weapon "*resembles* the gun I saw John have, in its *general appearance*. . . . it is my *impression* that it is [the same gun], and I have no doubt of it."[31]

The prosecution focused on Nicholas's motive for having Amasa Sprague murdered. New details were offered by witnesses who had testified in the previous trial. For example, both Charles Searle and Richard Knight, who had been prosecution witnesses at the earlier trial, testified again in Nicholas's trial as to what took place at the council meetings. At the first trial Searle had said that Amasa Sprague was present at the July meeting of the town council and had personally opposed the granting of a liquor license to Nicholas Gordon. The license was not granted. During the second trial, Searle stated that Amasa Sprague was ill and did not attend the July meeting, but that he did attend the August meeting and personally opposed Gordon's second attempt to have his liquor license renewed.[32] According to Searle's testimony, the town council had requested a written remonstrance from the opposers in June and that, he claimed, was the reason for the postponement of consideration until July. The minutes of the June town council meetings do not contain such a request for a written remonstrance.[33] What seemed a minor discrepancy of dates of no consequence was actually significant. In the previous trial the prosecution had left the implication that Nicholas had sent for his two brothers, John and William, *after* Amasa Sprague's opposition to renewal first surfaced. But Nicholas would have had to make arrangements some time earlier, certainly by the end of May, to have his family arrive in Boston by the end of June or beginning of July. Furthermore, he did not merely send for the two brothers, but for the whole family, consisting of four additional individuals.

In March 1843, when "a large number of females of Cranston" signed a petition "praying for the Council not to grant licenses for retailing strong liquors in said town," the council simply received it "for consideration at a future meeting."[34] Females, temperate or intemperate could not vote. But the temperance movement in Rhode Island, as elsewhere, was aggres-

sively campaigning for a statewide ban on the retail sale of liquor. In April
the Cranston Town Council, bowing to pressure from the local temperance group, had passed a resolution requesting an advisory vote from the
town's freemen on whether to continue "granting Licenses for keeping
Tavern and retailing wines and strong liquors." Despite growing opposition from temperance groups like the one composed of Cranston women,
the Cranston Town Council continued to grant such licenses because the
freemen of the town, all males, voted in the annual town meeting to allow
the council to do so.[35] Amasa Sprague's opposition to liquor licenses was
highly selective. He shared with other textile manufacturers like Zachariah Allen a firm belief that it was the duty of his workers to remain sober
and productive. To be fair to Amasa Sprague, a drunken or inattentive
operator on the job could wreck expensive machinery in no time at all,
especially in a print works, and Gordon's tavern was the closest one to the
print works and the one Sprague's workers would be likely to patronize
during the workday. When Sprague's representatives appeared at the
June 25 meeting opposing Gordon's license, the councilmen knew they
had a problem, but like many officials they also knew there was no
problem so controversial that it couldn't be postponed by the simple
expedient of declaring the remonstrance defective. *All* the other applicants were granted licenses at the June and July meetings.

Searle's testimony in Nicholas's trial was that the council rejected the
remonstrance at the *July* meeting "because part of the names were signed
with a pencil, and because some of the signers were Queen Victoria's
subjects," meaning they were Irish immigrants who were ineligible to
petition. Nothing like that happened according to the official minutes of
the meeting:

> The application of Nicholas S. Gordon . . . being again taken into consider-
> ation by this Council, objection is made to granting said License by
> Charles F. Searle, and a Petition or Protest against granting the same,
> signed by a number of persons is presented to this Council, and after hear-
> ing the remarks of said Gordon in favour, and of others against granting
> said License, and upon due consideration, it is voted unanimously by this
> Council not to grant said license.

After the Council acted to deny Gordon a license, it also took the following
action:

Permission of this Council is asked for the Petitioners to withdraw their petition or Protest against granting license to N. S. Gordon. It is thereupon voted by this Council that said Petitioners have leave to withdraw their Petition or Protest.

Said Petition or Protest is withdrawn accordingly.[36]

According to Searle's testimony, Amasa Sprague's name headed the list.

Searle was an employee of Amasa Sprague, but he insisted he was not employed to assist the prosecution. He admitted taking an active part in the prosecution, but claimed it was because "I was bound to to [*sic*] do, the murdered man having been my employer." "Queen Victoria's subjects" were presumably Irish employees of Sprague. Whatever their personal feelings about Nicholas Gordon or about drinking, they probably felt they had little choice but to sign. As Searle made clear in his testimony, "Mr. Sprague gave orders that if his help didn't stop visiting Gordon's store, they must leave him."[37] What better way was there to show they were obeying Sprague's order than to sign his petition.

Richard Knight corroborated Searle's testimony about Sprague's opposition to granting Nicholas Gordon a liquor license, adding that Sprague did not consider Gordon a suitable man to have a license. At the August town council meeting Sprague said he and some of the council members had seen Gordon drunk. Gordon replied "that he had never had his wagon loaded with stones," suggesting sharp practices by Sprague. Knight professed not to know what this meant, but Sprague did, and addressing the council, he said, "gentlemen this is slander it has nothing to do with this question, we will settle that between ourselves."[38]

Knight was very specific about the quarrel over the license, but he was allowed to testify to some vague, unspecified "difficulty" between Sprague and Gordon at the April 5, 1843, town meeting. The meeting was mainly devoted to the election of local and state officials. Nicholas Gordon had been declared a freeman and eligible to vote at town meetings by reason of his owning unencumbered, freehold property in excess of $134 in August 1842. Sprague and Gordon were in political opposition and the "difficulty" between them at the town meeting may have been no more (and no less) than a disagreement on issues and influence in local politics. However, the later argument between Gordon and Sprague was over the issue of the liquor license. The prosecution, having established that a public quarrel had occurred between Amasa Sprague and Nicholas Gordon in the summer of 1843, called further witnesses to develop its theory that Gordon's hatred of Sprague, engendered by the quarrel, constituted his motive for murder.

The first witness following Richard Knight, Hardin Hudson, repeated his testimony of the earlier trial that Nicholas Gordon would have his revenge upon Amasa Sprague. He added to his testimony in this trial that Nicholas told him "he had built an addition on his house with the intention of making that his business and it was just as bad as taking bread out of his mouth." Job Wilbur, however, who had reluctantly admitted in the first trial to having had a "difficulty" with Nicholas, was eager in the second trial to suggest that he and Amasa Sprague had stood in equal jeopardy from Gordon: "have heard that he said he would put Amasa Sprague and myself out of the way." He knew it because Ben Kit, the village fool, had told him so a few days before the murder.[39] The difficulty was that Sprague's workers would go to Wilbur's tavern, get drunk, then go to Gordon's store; Nicholas had been concerned he would then be accused of getting the Sprague workers drunk, having served them without a license.

A new witness, Paul Wheelock, was allowed to testify vaguely that he had heard Nicholas say "he would come up with him [Sprague] or something like that." The prosecution had wanted Susan Field on the stand that morning, but she was absent and an officer with "a writ of attachment" was sent to summon her to court. The court had to adjourn before noon because of her absence.

Susan Field had been an important witness against the Gordons in the first trial, the prosecution depending almost entirely on her to establish Nicholas's motive and to connect him to the coat found near the murder scene. In this second trial she shared the spotlight with many other witnesses testifying against him. Her testimony on direct examination apparently was almost entirely a repetition of her testimony in the previous trial; the *Transcript* published none of it. On cross-examination she launched into a long repetition of her testimony given during direct examination. More new facts about her life emerged than new facts about the Gordons.

We learn by implication that Susan Field's parents were separated, if not divorced. She was living with her father in Cranston when she first became acquainted with Nicholas Gordon. Later she lived with her mother, about a mile or more from the Gordons. Yet she had testified in the earlier trial that she went to the Gordon store frequently, as much as three times in one day, just to buy her mother a spool of thread or a needle or some such item. She moved to Providence in August 1843, living at Susan P. Gardner's on Benefit Street. The "arrangement" she had with Mrs. Gardner was, so to speak maternal: "I did not receive any particular wages; when I wanted anything she buys it for me however much it may cost."[40]

Susan Field's testimony remained damaging against Nicholas Gordon. She positively identified the coat as belonging to Nicholas and worn by both John and Nicholas. She testified the she frequently heard him make threats against Amasa Sprague, saying "he would run him through as soon as he would a snake." She repeated her testimony that Nicholas controlled his brothers, "by control, I mean that he had influence over them; they did what he told them to."[41]

The attorney general, however, did not depend on Susan Field's testimony alone to establish motivation. Both before and after her testimony, witnesses testified to Nicholas's threats or his anger against Amasa Sprague. Thadeus Manchester, for example, testified that he dropped into the store the morning before the day of the murder and asked to be served a drink, but he was told he could not be served because Gordon had lost his license. According to Manchester, Nicholas "either said we shall have Amasa Sprague out of the way, or, we shall put him out of the way next council day, I can't say which, I thought Mr. Sprague was a council man."[42] Another witness, Giles James, asked Nicholas Gordon to serve him some brandy because he was "unwell." Mr. James's simple request, made many times in the past, whether he was ill or not, elicited a tirade from Nicholas in August 1843.

> He said he could not sell me any, Amasa Sprague, a damned Algerine, had taken away his license; and before another year he [Amasa Sprague] would not be at the Town Council of Cranston, to say whether he should have a license or not. Said the store was all he had to depend upon for a living; that he could not work and a license was all he had to depend on, and he'd have satisfaction. Seemed to be very mad, slapped his fist down on the counter. . . .[43]

James then testified that he had warned Amasa Sprague of Nicholas Gordon's anger, suggesting it would be better to let him have the license, or else buy him out.

Although his testimony reinforced the theory that Nicholas Gordon's anger was murderous, James also testified to the fact that on the night of the murder he was in Mathewson's tavern when the subject on everybody's mind, the murder, was brought up by someone. Nicholas was present and, according to James, "said he was sorry for it; he got his living by trading with Mr. Sprague's help." Michael O'Brien, who was also present, "said he was glad of it. Nicholas told O'Brien not to talk so, the folks didn't like it; and said if he talked so, he [Nicholas] would not stay with him."[44]

Susan Field, whose testimony had been interrupted to allow Giles James to testify, returned to the witness stand to complete her testimony. She had had time to reconsider her past and now testified that four or five years ago she was living not in Cranston but in North Providence, several miles distant. About two years later she had gone to live with a family in Providence, and she had only "staid [sic] awhile" from about May through July 1843 at her mother's in Cranston.

Yet if she was contradictory about her own past, she was definite and specific about domestic details in the Gordon household. Nicholas's coat had black buttons and holes in it like the coat in evidence; on the day he arrived, John Gordon had worn "a pair of ribbed pantaloons; much worn, butternut color I should call them," the same pair in evidence at the trial. Her observations about Nicholas's garden that spring and summer lent authenticity to her testimony:

> I recollect being at Nicholas's store in May, and saw him setting out rair-ripes [sic?] in the garden. I saw there in June, he had sweet williams in his garden then, that was what he commenced joking me about his brother. I didn't think his brother looked like a very sweet William. It was in July that he joked me about his brother. There were sweet williams in his garden then.[45]

After Susan Field's testimony and the testimony of two witnesses who connected the coat described by Susan with the coat found in the swamp, the prosecution closed its case against Nicholas Gordon. Attorney William Potter's closing argument was not given in the *Transcript,* and one can presume he repeated the main points he had made in the first trial, with the focus this time on Nicholas Gordon.

On Friday morning, October 18, Attorney Rogers for the defense led off his case for Nicholas Gordon with Otis Stone who testified he "never knew anything bad about his character" in all the five or six years he had known him. But the evidence of the quarrel between Sprague and Gordon over the license preoccupied the defense as it had the prosecution. Rogers's strategy was to explain what Nicholas actually meant by his "threats" against Amasa Sprague, "and how he meant to 'come up with Mr. Sprague' or 'make him sorry for it.'" Attorney General Blake thereupon "proposed the introduction of the prisoner's previous declarations, to show the state of his mind previous to the murder, on the ground that the prisoner had no right to make testimony for himself."[46]

While the court considered the legal technicalities involved, Rogers called on witnesses to testify that Nicholas Gordon had never owned the coat found in the swamp, and on character witnesses like Jeremiah Baggott who testified that he had "always heard people speak well of Nicholas Gordon." On cross-examination Baggott was asked where Gordon came from; he replied he didn't know, but "when he came to Cranston [I] supposed he came from Ireland."[47] Evidently the prosecution had been hoping to tie Nicholas Gordon to the place name Tipperary which was printed on the scrap of newspaper found in the pocket of the coat.

By the afternoon session the court had made its ruling; it was apparently in favor of the defense, for the prosecution introduced no previous declarations, and the defense went ahead with its version of what happened at the town council meetings. Defense witness Charles Godwin described what happened at the August town council meeting when Nicholas again applied for a license:

> Mr. Sprague was present and objected, said the neighborhood was opposed to it, said he had seen him [Nicholas Gordon] drunk, had seen him kiss a negro. Gordon replied that he never had his waggon loaded up with stones on the public highway. There was a good deal of confusion. Gordon said as soon as he got a chance to speak, if his character was not as good as Mr. Sprague's he would give that pencil, holding up a pencil in his fingers. . . .[48]

The next witness, Olney W. Arnold, testified that at the same meeting Amasa Sprague said:

> he [Nicholas Gordon] was not a proper person; that he kept the worst house he had ever known in that town; that he had gambling in his house, the men who went there had lost their money; that nine tenths of the neighbors were opposed to his having a license; I do not despise him, said

Mr. Sprague, because he is an Irishman,—But he is the worst Irishman I have ever known in this country or any other.

This tirade had immediately followed the president of the town council's explanation to Nicholas that he could not have a copy of the remonstrance because it had been withdrawn, and that therefore "his character stood before the council just as it had done before the remonstrance."[49]

Another witness, Peleg Headly, testified that a few days later Gordon "did not threaten Mr. Sprague [,] said he didn't know as he should take out a license if they would let him"; and indeed, Headly "never heard him speak of Mr. Sprague in anger or unkindly." Seneca Stone, a former town council member, testified that after the confrontation at the council meeting Gordon had said he "intended to have Mr. Sprague put under bonds. He told me he spoke to a lawyer about it who advised him to drop it because Mr. Sprague was an influential man."[50] Thus when Nicholas said he would make Amasa Sprague "sorry" he ever impugned his character, he could have had in mind legal reprisal. Another witness, Arnold A. Stone, testified that Nicholas's "threat" was against the council, not Sprague: "he said the town council was influenced by Amasa Sprague, and that he and any other man could not obtain a license without he was willing, and spoke of turning out the council. Never heard him threaten Mr. Sprague." The threat, in other words, was to elect a new council not beholden to the Spragues. Two weeks after Stone's testimony, on November 2, the Cranston Town Council voted that N. S. Gordon be removed from the list of voters qualified to vote for electors of the president, vice president of the United States as well as from the general list of voters qualified to vote for town officials and the list of persons entitled to impose tax or expend money.[51] The council's action was legally correct, since Gordon's right to vote depended on owning real property *unencumbered* by debt. He had had to borrow money to pay for his defense, using his property as security.

Other witnesses testified that Nicholas Gordon blamed his fellow Irishmen more for the loss of his license, presumably because they signed the remonstrance, than he did Amasa Sprague. Indeed, one witness, Edward King, testified that on the night of the murder Nicholas defended Amasa Sprague against the tirade of the firebrand Dorrite Michael O'Brien. According to King, on hearing that Sprague had been murdered, supposedly shot to death, "O'Brien said he did not care if Mr. Sprague, and every other Algerine was shot to hell. Nicholas told him he ought not to say so . . . told O'Brien he was a very hard hearted man, to wish the death of such a man, who employed so many men. That he got most of his custom from Mr. Sprague's works which was the only support of his mother and himself."[52]

Saturday morning, the final day of testimony, Attorney Rogers called only one witness, Otis Stone, who lived next door to Nicholas and knew him well, having been in the habit of going to Nicholas's store often, as much as two or three times a day. Stone testified he had "never heard him speak about Amasa Sprague in connexion with his license. Never saw him wear the coat found in the swamp."[53] The difficulty for the defense strategy was the necessity of relying on testimony from witnesses who could only deny that they had heard Gordon speak hostile words against Sprague or that they had ever seen him wear the coat. Prosecution witnesses had made positive statements that Gordon had spoken with hostility and that they had seen him wear the coat found in the swamp.

On Friday afternoon, October 18, one of the final witnesses for the defense had been James Stratton. He had been a surprise witness in the earlier trial, providing the defense with an alternative theory of the murderer as the third man with a gun seeming to stalk Amasa Sprague. Again, Stratton was definite in his description that the man was larger and taller than John Gordon. His testimony was then corroborated by Francis M'Clocklin, but M'Clocklin could not swear to whether the man had a gun, only that he "heard the report of a gun" afterwards. Stratton's testimony was important to the defense for it needed to prove that John Gordon might be innocent, that there was another man with a gun at the scene of the crime, and therefore Nicholas Gordon did not incite his brother to do murder.

In rebuttal, on Saturday morning, Blake recalled Stratton, who vigorously denied he told William Sprague or any other person that the man with the gun he had seen near the scene of the crime had been so far away "that I could not form any opinion as to his size." Stratton was immediately followed on the witness stand by Charles Searle, faithful employee first of Amasa and now of William Sprague, who in effect called Stratton a liar:

I heard James Stratton tell Mr. [William] Sprague that he could not tell the size of the man whom he saw on the brow of the hill by Dyer's bridge. He

95

said he had on a blue coat; but that he could not tell anything about his size or height. Mr. Sprague asked him with reference to both these particulars.[54]

The jury would understand that Searle would not testify as he did without the approval of William Sprague. Furthermore, Sprague was sitting right there in the courtroom listening to Searle testify. It was, as the attorney general obviously wished, Stratton's word against Sprague's. Sprague wanted no suggestion that he had in any way suppressed vital evidence that would have raised a reasonable doubt about John Gordon's guilt or about Nicholas Gordon masterminding the plot to murder Amasa. William Sprague wanted what the prosecution wanted—a clear conviction.

The attorney general might have ended his case on a strong note with Searle's testimony. But instead he closed the rebuttal with two witnesses who had nothing to add to the case except derogatory hearsay. The first witness, Thomas Derry, an Irishman, testified, "I don't know anything about Nicholas Gordon, only I heard it said he was present at the murder of a teamster on Warren bridge[.] That's all I know." This testimony was so patently malicious that Attorney Rogers did not bother to cross-examine for the defense. Why Blake put Derry on the stand is puzzling; perhaps he wanted to show that not all Irishmen favored Gordon. The final witness in rebuttal, Benjamin Cozzens, was a lawyer, cotton manufacturer, and calico cloth printer. Cozzens testified, "[I] know something of N. S. Gordon. Have known him something more than three years. Known nothing with reference to his general character. From what I have heard of him with reference to a particular transaction at my print works should consider it very bad." On cross-examination he had to admit that he "knew nothing of this particular transaction but by hearing."[55] It is difficult to understand why Benjamin Cozzens would lend himself to that kind of hearsay testimony under oath. The best that can be said for him is that as a Yankee and a fellow cotton manufacturer he was showing solidarity with his kind.

There was no final surprise testimony on either side, just the dregs of hearsay and gossip on the prosecution side and an attempt by the defense to assure the jury that Nicholas owned a gun, not the murder weapon, but one that he kept in his bedroom as late as September 1843. There was no last-minute witness whose testimony would assure the acquittal of Nicholas Gordon. Yet there was one witness waiting to testify that Saturday morning who was never called by Rogers. William Gordon had been absent on Friday, the day when most of the defense witnesses testified. Still, he was there on Saturday. Instead, the attorneys for Nicholas Gordon closed their case; Samuel Currey completed the opening argument and Jonathan Rogers presented the closing argument. It was now up to Chief Justice Durfee to instruct the jury, and for the jury to decide.

On the surface, Chief Justice Durfee's instructions to the jury seemed to be a more balanced statement than his charge to the jury in the first trial. At least there was no overt suggestion as to which group of witnesses—Yankees or Irishmen—the jury should believe. Yet built into Durfee's charge was the court ruling that admitted the record of John Gordon's conviction as prima facie evidence of Nicholas's guilt. Throughout his statement to the jury Chief Justice Durfee came back to the point that John Gordon had been found guilty of the murder, and John Gordon was "one of the persons whom the prisoner [Nicholas Gordon] is charged with having stirred up, moved and incited to the deed."[56]

Although William Gordon was also specifically mentioned in the indictment charging Nicholas as an accessory before the fact to the murder, no reference was made by Durfee to the fact that William had been acquitted. No instructions or even the hint of a suggestion was forthcoming on how the jury should weigh that fact—did it weaken the prosecution's case against Nicholas, who was charged with stirring up, moving, hiring, counselling, abetting, and procuring William as well as brother John? It was John, John, John—he committed the murder, a fact not to be controverted. That the same motivation, the same words had *not* incited William to murder went unmentioned. The jury would have to decide whether Nicholas's "threats[,] declarations and conduct can be explained according to the ordinary laws of human action without coming to the conclusion that he is guilty of inciting John as charged in the indictment."[57] If the answer is yes, the jury must acquit; if the answer is no, the jury must convict.

The jury wrestled with this simple question for sixteen hours, rather than the seventy-five minutes it took the first jury to find John guilty and William innocent. In the end the jurors came to no decision, hopelessly deadlocked, eight for conviction, four for acquittal. Through their foreman, the members of the jury declared to the court their inability to agree upon a verdict. They were dismissed and a new trial was ordered.[58]

Four days later, the death of Samuel Y. Atwell, Esq., was announced in the *Transcript*. In the same issue a reporter summarized the trial: it had taken one hundred witnesses and eight days for the jury to reach its inconclusive verdict. "No criminal trial," the reporter declared, "in this or any other community, excited a more general interest, and seldom has any cause been contested with more zeal and earnestness by opposing Counsel."[59] Samuel Atwell lived long enough to learn the indecisive result of Nicholas Gordon's first trial, but not long enough to learn the final fate of John Gordon.

CHAPTER SIX

The Execution of John Gordon

William Gordon, having been acquitted and discharged on April 17, 1844, was a free man, but he was an unhappy and disturbed man. Friends assumed his emotional state was the result of anxiety he felt for his brothers John and Nicholas. Both his brothers were held incommunicado from him. Despite the fact that William had been married and was now a widower and father of a seven-year-old daughter, he depended on Nicholas as the head of the family. The prosecution had emphasized this relationship of both William and John to Nicholas in order to prove conspiracy. The defense argued the independence of every man's mind on such grave moral matters as the taking of another person's life. Yet it had also argued in its motion for arrest of judgment against John Gordon until after Nicholas's trial that "the paternal relation between the prisoner and Nicholas S. Gordon was really the controlling factor, from which the evidence affecting John, derived all its relevancy and force" (*Trial*, 81). In other words, if Nicholas was acquitted, John was innocent also.

After the end of Nicholas's first trial, Simon Mathewson, one of the jurors, decided on the spur of the moment to make a detour to Spraguesville, taking the Johnston road. He was accompanied by his employee, Lewis Chapman. It was only a mile out of his way, and he felt "a strong desire to see the scene of the murder and the neighboring grounds." A half mile from Fenner's tavern he and Chapman were overtaken by a wagon containing three men, one of whom was William Gordon.[1]

That Simon Mathewson and William Gordon should meet at that time and place was not an extraordinary coincidence, since William now lived in Nicholas's house and was on his way home from work. But what came from this meeting had unexpected results for the still unfolding tragedy. Mathewson mentioned he was on his way to view the scene of the crime and requested that one of the three men accompany him and Chapman "to point out to us the several places and objects referred to in the trial." William volunteered to go. Approaching the footbridge, Mathewson revealed that he considered John innocent, but he was not so sure of Nicholas because he owned a gun, and if it was not the murder weapon, then where was it? At the mention of the gun, William became very agitated and broke into tears, insisting that Nicholas's gun was *not* the murder weapon.

All this is revealed in an amazing document, a signed affidavit, which to all intents and purposes amounts to a confession by William Gordon that he had concealed vital evidence in a murder case in which he and his two brothers stood accused. This concealment took place on the evening of January 1, 1844, after Nicholas and John had been arrested, but before William had been detained. Yet it was not until nearly ten months later, after Nicholas's trial, that William told anyone other than his brother John. (He probably told John during their trial, which led to John's accusation of betrayal when the verdict was announced, even though John had agreed no one else should be told.) Not until the encounter with Mathewson did William reveal the full details of what he had done. What is perhaps even more amazing is that the story was not made public until February 10, 1845, just four days before the scheduled execution of John Gordon, more than a year after the concealment. Having told a stranger the full story of his having hidden the evidence, William then asked Mathewson not to disclose what he had done, to keep it secret until Nicholas's second trial.

It was a tragic series of misconceptions, misjudgments, and mistakes that persuaded William to withhold the fact that he had found and then hidden Nicholas's gun, the gun he had never denied owning, the gun Nicholas, who recognized the necessity of producing and handing it over to the authorities, insisted to Dr. Cleaveland was still in the store behind an oil can. Neither Dr. Cleaveland nor anyone else searching the store ever found it.

New Year's Day 1844, being a Monday, was a work day like any other day, and William was working at O'Brien's tailor shop in Providence. A shoemaker came in with the news that Amasa Sprague had been murdered, but William did not believe him or the others who came into the shop with rumors of the murder until his brother Nicholas arrived about noon and verified the fact.[2] Nicholas wanted William to spend New Year's

Day with the family in Spraguesville, but O'Brien would not let him off work until dusk. By the time William got home his brothers Nicholas and John had been arrested and taken away, and his mother and daughter were the only ones left at home. Restless, William decided to go into the store "without any motive or purpose" in mind, but he found the door to the shop locked on the shop side: "I then turned and opened the door of the room on the right hand of the room in which I was and on entering saw Nicholas's gun standing in the corner of the room on the right of the door."

William had been in the United States for only six months. In Ireland very few people of his religion and social class possessed guns, and he believed that the discovery of a gun in a suspect's house during a search by authorities investigating a shooting would be "enough to insure a conviction." He decided "it would be greatly to [his] brothers' advantage to conceal the gun." He said nothing to his mother and took the gun straight up to the attic, hiding it under the floor boards. His reflexive actions were understandable, but it was the worst thing he could have done. The second worst thing he could have done was to hide Nicholas's small pocket pistol as well, and he did that the next morning when he discovered the pistol on a top shelf in the kitchen closet, concealing it under the floor boards in the attic in a different spot, again saying nothing to his mother.

One must wonder at the kind of search made by Deputy Sheriff Potter and his assistant Daniel Chafee since they found neither the gun nor the pistol, which, while not exactly out in the open, were in no sense hidden. They were able to find a bayonet and a sword in the attic, but not a gun standing by itself in the corner of a room or a pistol on a shelf in the kitchen closet. Obviously, they were not expecting to find a gun openly standing in a room (the murder weapon had not yet been found, only a piece of it). Chafee had testified that in searching the house he particularly looked for a gun. Was it that he was looking for a broken gun, and therefore did not see or ignored a whole gun standing in the corner of that room? Yet he testified that no gun was found, ever. A pistol had already been found at the murder scene. Had the assumption already been made, twenty-four or so hours after the murder, that the pistol was Nicholas Gordon's, and that therefore there was no need to look for a pistol in the house itself? An upper shelf in a kitchen closet is hardly a difficult place to search. Sheldon Knight, a Law and Order town council member who had voted to deny Nicholas his liquor license, looked under a bed and found John Gordon's boots, but no one seemed to think of searching the closet shelves in the kitchen. Either the search was an inept and prejudicial one that looked only for evidence *against* the Gordons, ignoring anything that might tend to prove them innocent, or William Gordon's sworn statement was a complete fabrication from beginning to end.

Assuming that William's affidavit is generally truthful and factual, one is struck by the irony that had the gun and pistol been produced rather than hidden, John and Nicholas as well as William might have been acquitted. The question that had obviously bothered the first jury was that if the Gordons were innocent, why was the defense unable to produce Nicholas's gun if it was not the murder weapon? This question had also bothered Simon Mathewson during Nicholas's trial six months later. Granted that William acted impulsively and out of fear, why had he continued to withhold what he had done with the gun even when he himself was on trial for his life?

True, William states that he started out from Cranston on Tuesday morning, January 2, 1844, with the express purpose of seeing his brothers in prison and telling them what he had done. But when he reached Providence, he "was denied access to them." He walked back to Cranston again, arriving within a hundred yards of the Sprague mansion, not far from Nicholas's house, when he "was met by the Sheriff and his posse, who arrested [him] and committed [him] to Jail." Once jailed, William "was kept secluded from communication with any one but the officers of the prison for eight or nine days," until his appearance with his brothers before the examining magistrate. That the prison authorities kept the Gordon brothers apart is not surprising, since they had been arrested on suspicion of conspiracy to murder. The jailers wished to keep them from concocting a story.[3] Yet it is difficult to understand why William said nothing to Attorney John Knowles, who was permitted to see him "preparatory to the examination which was to be had the next day."

To understand why William might hide the gun is also to recognize why he kept vital information from defense counsel. William had acted instinctively to conceal the weapon from authority. John Knowles, although representing William, was an authority figure, a lawyer. To an immigrant in this country just over six months and unfamiliar with the law, Knowles was "one of them," not a fellow Irishman, certainly not family. He would have to speak first to Nicholas before revealing what he had done to a stranger who had to do with the law. If William had acted instinctively to hide the gun, he also knew instinctively that what he had done was unlawful. He did attempt, he states, "to speak with Nicholas, to inform him of the facts" while they were being questioned by the examining magistrate, but he was "checked by the officers in attendance and constrained to remove to a distance from him." He did not tell Knowles or any of the defense counsel during the trial. "I dared not," he confessed, "for I felt assured that they [the facts] would be regarded as evidence of my guilt."

Not until April, as they sat together in the courtroom did he tell his brother John what he had done. John understood the implications of what this concealment meant to his chances of acquittal, but he may have shared William's misconception of the law, believing that to disclose the facts would ensure William's conviction for murder. According to the affidavit, John did not use the information to save himself. He may have hoped that despite the odds the jury would find him innocent. When the verdict was announced, he could only lash out at the brother he loved: "It is you, William, that have hung me."

William was devastated by the verdict. On his conscience was the belief "that had I disclosed the facts known to me, he would have been acquited [*sic*] also," but that it was too late, now that the verdict was rendered. He believed, as he confessed, that he had selfishly saved himself and condemned a beloved brother to be wrongly executed for murder. John's courageous self-sacrifice was in sharp contrast to his selfish suppression of the evidence. William became so frantic in behavior and incoherent in speech that his friends thought him mad.

The most puzzling part of his statement has to do with his relationship with the defense counsel. On the one hand, he said, "I cannot say that I ever stated to any of the counsel of myself or my brother, that I knew aught of the gun or pistol." Yet at the same time he insisted that when asked by Mr. Rogers, Nicholas's defense counsel, he told Rogers he knew where the gun was hidden and that Attorneys Carpenter and Currey both knew the whole story. This contradiction is difficult to understand or accept.

A possible explanation of what actually happened is suggested by the testimony of Joseph Cole in the first trial. His statement that he told Richard Knight about William's alibi was contradicted by Knight's testimony that no such conversation took place. Cole may have conveyed his information by hint, by innuendo, by indirection, by shrug of the shoulder, wink of an eye, or nod of the head, and those used to such story telling (as Knight was not) would understand the drift of conversation. William had hoped and expected that Nicholas would be tried before him and John. He urged the defense counsel to arrange it that way because he "could put Nicholas in possession of facts that would clear him." William was so filled with what he had done he seems to have believed that to hint at the facts was sufficient. Everyone would know what he meant. Rogers presumably checked with Currey and Carpenter, but they must have told him there wasn't much to the story so that he pursued it no further.

William gave no plausible explanation as to why he never communicated what he knew to Nicholas after he himself was acquitted in April 1844. Possibly he was feeling so guilty about what he had done and so afraid of his older brother's reaction that he could not bring himself to tell him. Certainly there was an element of misjudgment on his part, as he hoped against hope that John's appeal for a new trial would be granted. Then he hoped against hope that Nicholas would be proved innocent during his trial, thereby necessitating a new trial for John. He himself would be the means by which Nicholas would be acquitted and John saved, for he did not doubt that he would be "called on when the Court sat to produce the gun and pistol, and testify in regard to them. Under this impression I attended the Court from day to day expecting to be called." Yet, he admitted, that on the day he might be called as a witness, he was absent.

Defense testimony occupied only part of Friday afternoon and Saturday morning. William was not a disinterested spectator or an unimportant witness. Yet he was *accidentally* absent from court. One can conclude that as the time approached he became more and more incapable of facing the enormity of what he had done. Rather than face the ordeal of public confession and probing cross-examination, he had fled. The defense counsel, probably dubious about the wisdom of putting William on the witness stand at all, apparently did not press the point and demand that the witness be found.

Simon Mathewson had impressed upon William the importance of his testimony to Nicholas's next trial and stressed that he "must not fail then to appear with the gun and the pistol." But Nicholas's next trial was not to begin until *after* February 14, 1845, the scheduled date for John Gordon's execution. William believed that from what he had heard from his friends and acquaintances, "John would be reprieved by the Legislature until after Nicholas should be tried again." William heard what he wanted to hear; his friends told him what they knew he wanted to hear. There was little hope that the general assembly, dominated by the Law and Order politicians, anti-Dorrite to a man and some of them anti-Irish to boot, would reprieve John Gordon.

The atmosphere in which the state legislature considered the reprieve petition was one bordering on hysteria. Rumors of an attempted escape by the Gordons were circulating. One such rumor surfaced in the *Transcript* on January 3, 1845, less than two weeks before the time the legislature took up the reprieve petition. The story was presented as a factual news report, not a rumor. "Attempt to Break Jail" was the headline:

> On new years night [exactly one year after the murder], John and Nicholas S. Gordon, attempted to effect their escape from the Providence county jail [which doubled as the state prison]. They had been provided with keys to open the doors of the rooms in which they were confined, and also the doors of the other apartments of the Jail.—The keys were supposed to have been furnished them by their brother William, who has been permitted to visit them, and has availed himself of the privilege nearly every day for some time past. . . .

The escape was supposedly detected by an off-duty watchman. A homey touch was added to the story for verisimilitude:

> The prisoners had been allowed to have a fiddle to amuse themselves with, and it was observed that evening to be played with more *force* than *good taste,* which led the watchman who had a nice ear for music, to listen more attentively, when he found that an accompaniment to the fiddle was being played upon the lock. . . .

The trouble with such rumors is that the storyteller does not let well enough alone but feels the necessity to expand and polish the story:

> Since writing the above, we learn that the key of the room in which Nicholas was confined was concealed in his cravat. The keys of the other rooms were found concealed about John and Nicholas. A saw was found concealed in the bunk, in the Gordons' room, with which they had sawed out a plank from the bunk to pry off the bars from the windows.

The state prison in Providence, about 1845

Embedded in the news story of the attempted escape was an editorializing paragraph calling upon the general assembly to improve prison security: "as it now is it is but an apology for a prison, and any person of moderate energy, can effect his escape, and without any very great exertion." Perhaps as a direct result of the *Transcript* story, the general assembly did pass a resolution "directing the keeper of the Providence County Jail to 'confine John Gordon, a convict now under sentence of death, and Nicholas S. Gordon, in separate cells, and in cells so distant that no communication can take place between them.' "[4] The indirect objective of the story was to put the legislature on notice that a reprieve would only increase the chances of an attempted escape. However, if the story had had any basis in fact, William Gordon would have been arrested on the spot. No such event occurred, and the general assembly considered the petition for a reprieve without reference to any attempted jailbreak.

The supporters of the petition for a reprieve—actually, a petition for a stay of execution until such time as Nicholas's second trial could be completed—were hardly pro-Gordon or antigallows. Fenner Brown of Cumberland led the argument in favor of the petition on the grounds that the delay of execution might facilitate the discovery of "the other person" concerned in committing the murder: "He believed that if this man [John Gordon] was guilty, his brothers must be guilty too."[5]

Wilkins Updike of South Kingstown led the opposition to the petition. Updike, a blunt and outspoken politician from the southern part of the state, was a shrewd and able lawyer of long experience. Descended of old Yankee stock, he was the opposite of the new immigrants. Rigid in his concept of law and order, he opposed attempts to abolish the death penalty. The petitioner had had a fair trial and was found guilty, he argued; hang him. Leniency could only lead to disregard for the law: "Nothing but the prompt enforcement of every law, and the inflexible opposition of the pardoning power, to every interference with the judgments of the Court, will save us from this calamity." To interfere would only be "opening a way of escape to the greatest criminals."[6]

Given the one-sided nature of the debate, the vote was surprisingly close, twenty-seven in favor and thirty-six against. The shift of five votes would have resulted in passage. Four days later, a resolution from the senate for the establishment of a joint committee of both houses to consider "a Petition of numerous citizens of Providence, for a suspension of the sentence of John Gordon" was rejected by a larger margin. In the interim between the consideration of these two petitions the general assembly had been polarized politically by the previous debate on a bill to grant amnesty to Thomas Dorr from his life sentence at hard labor.[7]

Brown again led the argument for a stay of Gordon's execution, with Updike opposing. Representative Robert B. Cranston of Newport opposed the Gordon resolution on traditional grounds—a vigorous execution of the laws was necessary for the safety of society and the deterrence of criminals. Cranston was "sorry to see so much sickly sensibility" for a murderer. Representative Sylvester G. Sherman of North Kingstown suspected a plot by the antigallows adherents and "had no sympathy with these pretenders to unbounded philanthropy." The only surprise in the debate was the announcement by Representative Tourtellot that he wished to present a petition on the subject of capital punishment "headed by one of the jurors who sat upon the trial of John Gordon." The juror was unidentified, but obviously he had had second thoughts about the necessity of the death penalty, if not about the guilt of John Gordon. Tourtellot cited what he understood to be the opinion of Justice Staples "that as Nicholas Gordon might undertake to show the innocence of John, in order to prove his own, John would be still on trial." But both

Cranston and Updike denied this was Staples's opinion. Updike again was the most adamant against any delay in the execution of John Gordon. He admitted he "knew nothing about the prisoner. He had never read the evidence. Newspaper evidence was not to be relied upon. It was the appearance, the look of the witness which gave its force to testimony." Obviously Updike did not like the looks of Nicholas Gordon either, for he suspected "that it was Nicholas Gordon, not John, who had put forth this petition. He dreads the confession of his brother, and hopes to get an acquittal before the confession shall place it beyond his power to do so."[8] The vote to deny both the senate resolution and the juror's petition was thirty-nine to deny and twenty-one to accept.

It was not until February 6, nearly three weeks later, just eight days before the date of execution, that William told anyone else his secret. He had known since October, if not earlier, that he could not be tried again for the murder; Simon Mathewson had assured him of that. He seemed incapable of acting on his own initiative. It was almost in passing that he mentioned to his current employer, Patrick Brennan, "that it was hard that John should be hung upon the proof against him, when I had Nicholas's gun in my keeping all the while." Brennan told his neighbor, Lewis Devlin, who then told his brother John. John Devlin, after assuring himself that the gun was actually there under the floorboards as William said it was, urged William to set forth the facts in an affidavit. It was only then that William finally acted. On February 10, 1845, he appeared before the justice of the peace in the city of Providence "and made oath that the afore written affidavit by him subscribed, is true in all its parts." What thoughts were going through the mind of the justice of the peace at that moment are unrecorded, but his signature is clear: he was J. C. Hidden, the foreman of the jury that had found John Gordon guilty and William not guilty of the murder of Amasa Sprague.

William's affidavit was then attached to John Gordon's petition to James Fenner, the governor, for a reprieve "until his brother Nicholas shall have been again tried" and "until the end of the next session of the Assembly" so that he can "solicit from the Legislature of the State a consideration of his case" in the light of this new evidence. A covering letter from Defense Attorney John P. Knowles, dated 12:30 o'clock, February 10, and addressed to Governor James Fenner, stated that within the hour Knowles had learned from a friend "that the Judges of the Supreme Court are unanimously of opinion that John Gordon ought, as a matter of right, to be reprieved, until after a second trial of his brother Nicholas:—for on his trial, Nicholas assumes on himself the burthen of proving the innocence of John. He assumed this on his late trial, and as a Juror, Mr. Mathewson, informs me, the Jury disagreed upon John's case, rather than upon that of Nicholas."[9] In other words, the jury in Nicholas's trial had doubts that John Gordon was proven guilty by the evidence but felt that the evidence tended to prove Nicholas guilty, particularly the evidence of the gun. Mathewson himself in his affidavit indicated he had originally thought John innocent but Nicholas guilty because of the evidence of the gun. With the discovery of the gun hidden by William Gordon, Mathewson was convinced not only that John Gordon was innocent but that Nicholas was too.

Unfortunately for John Gordon the Rhode Island constitution placed a time limit, and a very brief one at that, on the governor's power to grant a reprieve after conviction. Having consulted Attorney General Blake to advise him on the law, Governor Fenner replied on the same day, February 10, that he had "no power to *reprieve*, excepting that which is given by Section 4 of Article 7, of the Constitution in the following words—'He [the governor] shall have power to grant reprieve *after conviction*, in all cases except those of impeachment, *until the end of the next session of the General Assembly*'—thus limiting the *exercise* of the power to a *specific term*" between conviction and the end of the next session of the general assembly. (Thomas Dorr's "People's Constitution" would have granted the governor unrestricted right to reprieve except in cases of impeachment; the clause "until the end of the next session of the General Assembly" was omitted from that document.)

In his reply to Knowles, Governor Fenner pointed out that four sessions of the general assembly had passed since John Gordon's conviction and two since sentence was imposed. John Knowles had obviously been hoping for an act of clemency based on a loose interpretation of the constitution. In his covering letter he had suggested that his unnamed friend had "reason to believe" the supreme court holds the opinion that the governor has the power to reprieve "notwithstanding that a session of the assembly had intervened between the day of sentence and the date of the application for a reprieve." Whatever his personal feelings and opinions on the matter, Governor Fenner denied John Gordon's petition on the grounds that he had no constitutional power to grant a reprieve under the circumstances. The execution remained set for February 14. Time had run out for John Gordon.

The appeal to the governor having failed, John Gordon's supporters promptly published William's affidavit concerning his hiding of Nicholas's gun. On the day set for the execution of John Gordon, the *Transcript* commented on the affidavit and John Gordon's petition to the governor for a stay of execution, suggesting that it is difficult to believe this was the same gun and if it was that William would have kept the fact concealed for so long. It seemed an improbable story, and the timing of the revelation seemed intended "to injure the position of Governor Fenner before the community."[10] With elections only six weeks away, the *Transcript* was certain the public distribution of John Gordon's petition in the form of a handbill was politically motivated. The *Boston Pilot,* on the other hand, reported editorially that John Gordon's execution was "untimely," and that "there seemed to be the strongest conviction of his innocence in all quarters."[11] Needless to say, the execution took place on schedule.

Rhode Island was the first state to abolish *public* executions, doing so in 1833, a year earlier than Pennsylvania. Although Rhode Island's list of capital crimes included arson, rape, robbery, burglary, and the second offense of sodomy as well as murder, there had been no executions from 1798 to 1831. But between June 1832 and January 1834 there were three hangings scheduled, which led to the abolition of public executions.[12] The application of the word "private" to hangings after 1833 was a relative term. Sixty persons were official eyewitnesses to the execution of John Gordon in 1845, but since the execution took place in the prison yard, there were additional eyewitnesses among the prisoners on that side of the prison, possibly including Thomas Dorr who had been spared the death penalty for treason by the 1798 revision of the criminal code. A large crowd of over a thousand people had gathered on a hill above the prison, although their view was restricted by a high fence built to prevent any kind of demonstration that could "excite a kind of bravado in the mind of the wretched man."[13]

The reporter for the *Transcript,* himself an eyewitness, described the execution as a "strictly private" affair. The fact that 250 people attended the "private" execution in Boston of John White Webster, a Harvard professor, in 1850 suggests that private did not mean limited to a handful of officials. But the abolition of public hangings in Rhode Island was not enacted out of deference for the prisoner or his family. A race riot had occurred in Providence in September 1831, triggered by the fact that an Irish sailor had been killed by a black man. A mob of white men, incensed by the killing, "went on a rampage, making no distinction between the residents, destroying property indiscriminately, and eventually threatening to loot banks and businesses in the area."[14] In the end, the state militia, after the mob had assembled again intent on rioting, fired on the crowd, killing four white men and wounding many others. Only then did the mob disperse.

The middle-class fear of social disorder by a mob gathered for the rites of execution had much to do with the abolition of public hangings. As Louis P. Masur observed, the agitation for private hanging "coincided with the emergence of a middle class that valued internal restraints and private punishments."[15] The blue ribbon committee investigating the Providence Riot of 1831 was composed entirely of middle-class men—bankers, lawyers, merchants, manufacturers. They emphasized in their report the threat to civil order that mob rule represented: "of all the evils that can be inflicted upon a civil society, that of a lawless and ferocious mob is the most capricious in its objects, the most savage in its means, and the most extensive in its consequences."[16] The fact that no less than three public executions—timed when potentially dangerous mobs might assemble—were scheduled within an eighteen-month period in 1832–33 led Rhode Island legislators to act quickly to change the law. If they needed a final impetus it came when a crowd estimated at ten thousand gathered to witness a public hanging near Providence in 1832.[17]

Of the sixty eyewitnesses to John Gordon's execution, some were there in their official capacity as officers or attending physicians and some were reporters, but others had been invited by the sheriff "to see that the execution was properly done."[18] In the context of a hanging, whether public or private, "properly done" referred not only to the physical execution but also to the moral and spiritual ritual of the ceremony leading to the repentance and redemption of the criminal. Ministers, merchants, and middle-class professionals were invited to witness the conversion of the criminal from sinner to penitent. As Masur observed in *Rites of Execution*, "an elite segment of society gathered at private executions to celebrate the extinction of vice now viewed as originating from within the community." Private executions "became a theatrical event for an assembly of elite men who attended the execution by invitation while the community at large was excluded."[19]

Central to the drama was the criminal himself who was expected to confess his guilt and beg forgiveness of God and society. This expectation is implied in the newspaper reporter's eyewitness account of John Gordon's execution, but John Gordon did not conform to the ritual of confession and remorse:

> I am here, at the place of execution—here in this terrible place, where, shortly, the life of a human being, a fellow man, is to be offered up, a sacrifice to the laws. I have seen him—the unfortunate man, who is soon to suffer—perhaps I should say, who has suffered so much, and whose sufferings are so soon to end. Pale and haggard, there is yet a look of composure, almost of innocence, in his countenance. Some ray of hope—the hope, perhaps, which his religion brings him—seems mingled with his despair. He does not look like a bad man—like a murderer. To me he seems more the image of a man of little mind, whose thoughts have been disturbed by a sudden and to him inexplicable accusation of crime and incarceration with felons, and who is trying to recover himself and understand his position. Imprisonment has worn him down; he is thin, pale, and evidently feeble in body. Mental torture—the torture of guilt, may have made him so—but I cannot look upon him as a man of intellect, and capable of much mental suffering. A kind of bashfulness in him, I would attribute more to lack of intellect and education than to a sense of guilt. It does not seem the reservedness of the conscience-stricken murderer.

At about ten o'clock, Nicholas and William were allowed to see their brother for the last time. The parish priest, Father John Brady, was already with John. They remained with him until eleven o'clock when the sheriff came for him. The *Transcript* reporter described the scene:

> Now comes the Sheriff; he enters John's cell, and adjusts his white robe and cap. He seems affected; while John is calm and composed as though nothing terrible was about to transpire. They leave the cell together, accompanied by the Priest. Nicholas and John meet on the corridor, and take a long farewell; what they say I cannot hear; but strange to say, John seems urging Nicholas to take courage and not be down-hearted. They part, and John, the Sheriff and the Priest, mount the scaffold in the prison yard.[20]

Father Brady's last words to John Gordon on the scaffold during those final moments before the execution, did not follow the expected ritual of platitudinous spiritual solace for a remorseful but guilty criminal. Instead, Father Brady was quoted by the *Transcript* as saying, "*Courage, Brother John, Courage!* you are about to join the immortal band of your countrymen, who have been sacrificed on the altar of superstition and prejudice."[21] The editor of the *Transcript*, Joseph S. Pitman, was highly incensed by this breach of the rites of execution:

> the priest who officiated on that occasion so far forgotten [*sic*] his duty to
> the State which protects him, as to make use of language calculated only to
> excite the worst feelings in all classes of society. He used that occasion to
> awaken in this community the worst feelings of the Irish population
> against the government of the State. No person who has watched the trial
> of John Gordon, can believe that he has suffered as a martyr to Catholi-
> cism. Yet such is the view which the Catholic priest would present to Gor-
> don's sympathetic countrymen. What his real object was we cannot say. But
> the only inference to be drawn therefrom is, that he desired to array Cath-
> olics against the Protestants, the Irish against the Americans. . . .[22]

The priest insisted his actual words had been: "Have courage, John; you are going to appear before a just and merciful Judge. You are going to join myriads of your countrymen, who, *like you,* were sacrificed at the shrine of bigotry and prejudice. Forgive your enemies."[23] The correction was printed in the *Transcript,* but the editor was not mollified.

John Gordon's response to Father Brady was "I do [forgive my enemies]. I forgive all my enemies, and persecutors. I forgive them for they know not what they do."[24] Editor Pitman was deeply offended by John's attitude of Christ-like martyrdom and innocence. He was also offended by an editorial in the *New World Weekly* (February 22, 1845) which criticized the Rhode Island legislature for not granting John Gordon's petition for a reprieve until after Nicholas's trial, since there was, the *New World* declared, "a strong probability of his innocence existing." The editor of the *Transcript* replied that John was guilty because he had not said he was innocent in his final words. He had not proclaimed his innocence in public, the editor argued, because he had already confessed his guilt to the priest and received absolution. If he had declared his innocence on the scaffold, his countrymen would have believed him, but "as he did not, they deem him guilty." For if he had lied and said he was innocent at the end, far from being absolved, he would have gone to hell. The only reason he did not publicly confess his guilt, the *Transcript* editor declared, was that "he would have brought to light some circumstances which would have convicted Nicholas. He was deterred from making a confession in the hope that Nicholas would be freed."[25]

John Gordon's final words—besides telling the sheriff, yes, he was ready—were "I hope all good Christians will pray for me" (*Full Report*, 55). This was not what some Protestants wanted to hear, and it went unreported in the *Transcript*. They wanted to hear John Gordon confess that he was guilty. They were willing to believe that misguided Papists would try to make him a martyr. They were willing to believe that die-hard Dorrites like the Reverend William S. Balch, the firebrand Protestant minister who had fled the state because of the sedition laws, would try to undermine the verdict, claiming that it was politically motivated, as the Dorr verdict had been. But they did not want to believe there had been a miscarriage of justice. As the reporter for the *Transcript* wrote, "We could look upon it in no other light than the vindication of the laws, which had been outraged, and regretted that the evil passions of men should have rendered such vindication necessary."[26]

The body of John Gordon was left hanging on the gallows for twenty minutes before being taken down and placed in a coffin inscribed simply, "John Gordon, Aged 29 Years." It was then delivered to his friends "to be conveyed to Cranston, to his brother's house." The coffin was carried past the *Transcript*'s office "attended by a large number of countrymen, and countrywomen of the unhappy murderer."[27] To reach Nicholas Gordon's house the entourage had to pass Amasa Sprague's house. Whatever the thoughts of those who accompanied the coffin past the Sprague mansion, John Gordon was beyond caring. His funeral was set for two days later, a Sunday.

The Irish in Providence became convinced of John Gordon's innocence after his execution, whatever their doubts before: "small squads of his countrymen, may be seen in our streets, seemingly absorbed in commenting on his horrible end, loudly, to each other, protesting that he was innocent of the crime, and denouncing those who condemned him.—All appear in considerable excitement."[28] Word of William's revelation about the hidden gun spread rapidly throughout the Rhode Island Irish community, and the failure of "those who condemned him" to show mercy and grant a reprieve until after Nicholas's second trial was deeply resented. However, there were no violent demonstrations in Providence after the execution, and in Cranston "no undue excitement" was reported.

The funeral procession itself was a quiet and orderly but impressive demonstration of community solidarity among the Irish. Over fourteen hundred friends and fellow countrymen followed the coffin to the North Burial Ground in Providence; many hundreds lined the streets along the route. More of them would have joined the procession, according to a contemporary eyewitness account, but dared not "for fear of losing their employment."[29] The funeral procession took thirty minutes to pass a particular intersection along the way. That the funeral was a political statement is evident in the fact that many of those who followed the cortege came from other towns and cities in Rhode Island and even from Massachusetts and Connecticut. Some were protesting a miscarriage of justice, believing John Gordon innocent. Others were protesting hanging as a punishment for murder. All were making a point as they followed John Gordon's remains across the Crawford Street Bridge in Providence. Instead of turning to follow North Main Street they continued up the hill to Benefit Street where they turned left to march along that street as an alternate route to the North Burial Ground a mile beyond the intersection of Benefit and North Main streets. John Gordon's body passed the rear of the state house where he had been tried and convicted. The procession went past the mansion of Sullivan Dorr, one of the eyewitnesses invited by the sheriff to see the execution. It passed the home of William Staples, the antigallows judge who had helped to hang him. Finally, just before reaching North Main Street, John Gordon's coffin passed the house of Susan Parr whose "inmate" Susan Field had done so much in her testimony to convict him. His last words may have forgiven all his persecutors; his funeral was a final petition that they not forget him.

CHAPTER SEVEN

Nicholas Gordon's Second Trial

Rhode Island politics shifted significantly in early April 1845. The national Democratic Party victory in 1844 had helped the Dorrite wing of the state party through patronage. The Rhode Island Democrats formed a coalition with dissident members of the Law and Order Party on the single issue of the liberation of Thomas Dorr from prison and the restoration of his civil rights without conditions. The Law and Order Party, composed mainly of conservative Whigs, had been weakened by its image of repression, hostility to reform, and judicial tyranny. Headed by Charles Jackson, a general assembly representative from Providence, the Liberation Party won the April gubernatorial election by a narrow margin.[1]

The Dorrite victory at the polls did not directly affect the second trial of Nicholas Gordon, which began the week after the election and appeared to be almost a replay of the first trial. The same prosecution team of Attorney General Joseph Blake (he had been reelected even though his party lost the gubernatorial election) and Attorney William Potter tried the case for the State. The same defense team of Jonathan Rogers and Samuel Currey defended Nicholas Gordon. The same judges presided over the case. Yet there was an indirect and important difference in the climate in which the two trials took place. The execution of John Gordon before the start of Nicholas Gordon's second trial had created more uneasiness about John's guilt, especially after the publication of William Gordon's affidavit about the gun. John Gordon had become a posthumous cause célèbre. "Soon pro and antigallow editors as far away as New York City, Utica, and Boston were decrying the death of an innocent man," according to Philip Mackey.[2] The Irish in Rhode Island viewed the execution as judicial murder and generally as an attack on them.

The second Nicholas Gordon trial began Monday morning April 7,

1845, with the questioning of potential jurors. Of nearly one hundred eligible jurors, fifty-six were disqualified as "having already formed or expressed opinions as to the guilt or innocence of the prisoner or his brother John." (Only twenty-two had been similarly disqualified in the first Nicholas Gordon trial.) Thirteen were disqualified by reason of "conscientious scruples," as opposed to only three in the previous trial, reflecting an upsurge of antigallows sentiment in Rhode Island as a consequence of John Gordon's execution. Two possible jurors were disqualified "on account of relationship to Mr. Sprague," and eleven, the same number as in the first trial, were peremptorily challenged by the defense counsel.[3]

One juror who was *not* peremptorily challenged by the defense was the foreman, Isaac Saunders, a cotton manufacturer. Yet when asked by defense counsel whether he had formed an opinion as to the guilt or innocence of the Gordon brothers, Saunders replied that he thought *if* John Gordon was guilty, Nicholas must be far more so. Despite this admission, the defense attorney did not have him disqualified.[4] This decision might seem a dereliction of duty on the part of the defense since the prosecution's case against Nicholas Gordon rested on John Gordon's guilt as prima facie evidence of Nicholas's guilt. The defense was taking a calculated risk in accepting Saunders since the corollary to his premise was that if John Gordon was innocent, then in all likelihood (though not necessarily, as the prosecution would be quick to point out) Nicholas must be far more so.

The prosecution's case was of necessity much the same as in the previous trial and the focus was again on Gordon's quarrel with Sprague and on his ownership of the gun and coat found at the murder scene. There were minor differences in William Potter's opening argument; in the second trial he emphasized that Gordon was "a foreigner" at a time when there was an influx of Irish immigrants into Rhode Island and was seen as a threat by some of the Anglo-Saxon Protestant natives of the area. Potter also emphasized that Gordon was a "keeper of a shop for the sale of intoxicating liquors" at a time when agitation for prohibition in the state was as ardent as the spirits. Because it was well over a year since the murder had occurred, the jury was taken to visit the scene of the crime the following morning, Tuesday, April 8.

The same witnesses presented the same circumstantial evidence against Nicholas Gordon. And if one of the familiar witnesses seemed less certain of his testimony and evidence given in the previous trials, there was another witness to reinforce the prosecution on that point. Abner Sprague, Jr., faltered and now admitted that there was no particular difference between the gun he saw John Gordon carrying and any other fowling piece that would enable him to identify the Gordon gun as the murder weapon. James Francis, on the other hand, insisted that the murder weapon was the same gun he had owned and sold to Nicholas Gordon through Tillinghast Almy's auction. "[I] am certain this is the same gun I owned," he declared without doubt upon cross-examination. However, the testimony of another prosecution witness on the gun backfired upon cross-examination. "The bore of the gun Nicholas had," Augustus Moffit admitted to Mr. Rogers, "was larger than the one in Court [the murder weapon]."[5]

A new witness, Nicholas Shreeve, was called by the attorney general to reinforce the testimony about Nicholas's hostility to Amasa Sprague over the license. Shreeve quoted Gordon as saying, "Amasa Sprague, God damn him, has prevented me from getting a license, and before another year, I'll be revenged on him, or I'll pay him for it." On cross-examination he admitted that at the time he thought it barroom talk, but on hindsight, when he heard that Amasa Sprague had been murdered, "it occurred to me that Gordon had *paid him*." Shreeve appeared to strengthen the prosecution's case, but he also revealed in direct testimony that the context of Gordon's statement was a very practical matter; Gordon had been "about to hire a tavern stand at the Crompton Mills" in Warwick, and needed to know if William Sprague controlled "the town of Warwick, like Amasa Sprague the town of Cranston." Amasa, Nicholas said, "used the Town Council there so that I can't get a license."[6] Apparently William Sprague did, for Nicholas never applied for a license from the Warwick Town Council, but this does suggest that he was seeking practical alternatives rather than brooding about Amasa Sprague's opposition. It suggested also that Gordon's threat as spoken in the presence of Nicholas Shreeve reflected an intention to seek *political* revenge rather than commit murderous assault.

Testifying again about the Cranston Town Council confrontation between Sprague and Gordon, Charles G. Searle mentioned on cross-examination that John Watts, a day laborer at the Sprague plant, had been dismissed because he had gone to Gordon's store. Susan Field stated that Nicholas had said, "God damn the man that took [my] license away—[I'll] have his life," in the presence of his brother John. Yet the final prosecution witness, Benjamin Potter (identified as Amos Potter in Nicholas's first trial), seemed to weaken the prosecution testimony regarding Nicholas's motivation. He testified, as he had in the first trial, that he had met Nicholas Sunday night about eight o'clock opposite Richard Knight's boardinghouse. Nicholas was in the company of a tall man. Obviously what the prosecution wanted was a repetition of the testimony given at the first trial, that Nicholas had felt compelled to say "he didn't *help* kill him." Instead Potter reported that Nicholas said, "Thank God I didn't kill him. I wasn't there." He said this along with being "sorry for Mr. Sprague's death." Furthermore, Potter revealed that Nicholas said, "I'm pretty drunk this evening," an obvious explanation as to why he could not go to Sprague's house to pay his last respects.[7] The *Providence Journal* had been quick to find the Gordons guilty for not going to the house; think what the *Journal* would have said had the Gordons shown up drunk.

All in all, compared to the earlier trial, the prosecution's case against Nicholas was less vigorous and less clear. William Potter seemed almost to admit this in his closing argument when he said to the jury that "he felt he had not a clear idea of the evidence, notwithstanding he had twice been through it."[8] Potter's ploy was a rhetorical device to recapitulate the evidence, yet underneath there seemed to be a weariness in presenting the same argument for the third time.

In contrast, Rogers for the defense was vigorous in his cross-examination and effective in presenting his side of the case. Besides cross-examining witnesses about Nicholas's gun, he carefully cross-examined Horatio N. Waterman and got him to admit that, although there was only one track from Hawkins' Hole near where the coat and gun were found to the Gordon House, "there were forty tracks across the bog meadow" that were not measured as part of the evidence. John De Merritt stated that he didn't measure the other tracks because they appeared older; yet he admitted upon cross-examination that he could not tell the difference in appearance between the tracks made Sunday afternoon (the time of discovery of the murder) and those made Monday morning. At the same time he observed that the measure he used was never put in evidence at any of the trials because "it got broken and one piece of it lost" long before the first trial.[9] These were details, but they brought out the ineptness and bias of the murder investigation.

Attorney Rogers's question about the "age" of the tracks was not asked in idle curiosity. It was made to set the stage for two defense witnesses, William Tately and William Downey, who admitted they had made tracks between the swamp and Gordon's house on Monday when they had taken a short cut from Hawkins' Hole. They were curious about the murder and wanted to find out what had happened. Downey actually joined the searchers looking for weapons, and then he made tracks to the Gordon house, passing close to the rear door, wearing a pair of light boots. "By God, Bill," Tately said to him during the previous trial when they heard the evidence, "John Gordon was convicted on your footsteps." Downey said he was summoned to court to testify the next day, "but 'twas too late."[10]

Rogers's strategy was to aggressively undermine the circumstantial evidence presented by the prosecution. Instead of just complaining about the circumstantial nature of the government's evidence against the Gordons, Samuel Currey in his opening argument suggested that everything the government had sought to prove is "not at all inconsistent with the innocence of the prisoner."[11] To do this Rogers followed a twofold attack on the prosecution's case: first, in cross-examining prosecution witnesses, he explored weaknesses and uncertainties in the evidence, such as the testimony about the gun and the tracks; and second, in presenting its own witnesses, the defense sought to give an alternative explanation for the evidence, such as the tracks made by Tately and Downey, or to present witnesses who contradicted prosecution testimony.

The most vigorous attack by Rogers was against the prosecution's interpretation of motivation. First of all, he attempted to prove that three of the seven members of the town council voted against the renewal of *all* liquor licenses, not just Gordon's, and that therefore Amasa Sprague's opposition to Nicholas's license was not the sole reason for his losing it. The temperance movement had apparently made an impact on some of the council members. The defense counsel had obviously done its homework, but the court remained consistently biased and ruled in favor of the prosecution that such testimony was inadmissible. That being the case, in order to present its own interpretation of Gordon's "threats" against Sprague, the defense needed first to break down the prosecution's testimony.

Caleb Arnold, a Providence shoemaker, was called as a defense witness to contradict Giles James's testimony that Nicholas had made threats against Amasa Sprague. Arnold said he was with James but denied that

Gordon had made any threats, and he said James had not even spoken to Gordon. Here again was one man's word against another's, but it was nonetheless a direct contradiction of what a prosecution witness claimed Nicholas had said rather than merely just another defense witness saying he had never heard Gordon threaten Sprague.

On cross-examination Arnold inadvertently revealed how the Sprague family had gone about collecting evidence against the Gordons: "Mr. Rice came out to inquire if I heard any [threats by Nicholas Gordon against Amasa Sprague], and [inquired of] Mr. James several times."[12] Rice was Amasa and William Sprague's brother-in-law, and on this occasion at least he had assumed the role of both sheriff and prosecutor, putting together evidence that would help convict the Gordons and discarding anything (such as Caleb Arnold's testimony) that would undercut the conspiracy theory that Nicholas incited his brothers to murder Amasa over the loss of the liquor license.

The attorney general's "star" witness regarding Nicholas's threats was again Susan Field. Rogers called her as a hostile witness to ask one question: Did she tell anyone during the last term of the court that in the John Gordon trial she had testified "to what she knew nothing about," and for that reason she had not wanted to testify again in the first Nicholas Gordon trial? (Susan Field had to be summoned by an officer before she appeared to testify in that trial.) She vigorously denied she had told anyone such a thing; to have said otherwise would have been to admit to perjury. Attorney Rogers then called Ezra Going (or Gowan). Susan Field, he testified, "came to my house just before the trial of Nicholas Gordon last Fall, said she had sworn to that about the Gordons that she knew nothing of. Before another session of the Court she should be off. I advised her to go before the Court and make an acknowledgment if she had told what was not true. . . ."[13] Blake could not change Going's testimony on cross-examination, and Going added that his wife was present when Susan Field made the damaging admission.

Susan Field also claimed that Lydia Going was her "sister," but Lydia herself denied any such relationship. Susan Field, Lydia testified, "came to me with Mrs. Parr. She said she had told what she knew nothing about, and didn't want to tell it over again. She wouldn't go to the Court House again. I have known her ever since she was a child, was brought up with her."

On cross-examination Lydia Going stuck to her statement and added that Mrs. Parr told Susan Field not "to come" to court, for "if she did, she shouldn't stay in her house any longer," meaning presumably if she again perjured herself.[14]

Susan Field, as a rebuttal witness, had recovered her aplomb and returned to the attack:

> Never told Mr. and Mrs. Going anything about my testimony, I told Lydia I was going to Court, she said not go, I had got a great many enemies by going, I answered that I couldn't die but once. I didn't come when summoned at the former trial because I was hindered from coming, I heard that this gentleman (pointing to Mr. Curry [sic]) said if I came again my oath shouldn't weigh much, he would stoop to the lowest means to prevent it, others persuaded me not to come on account of these threats.

Susan Field knew well the value of attack when on the defensive, and she used every weapon in her arsenal:

> Saw Lydia [Mrs. Going] when she came out of jail, said she used to talk with John Gordon through the grates. She told me not to come to Court, for Mr. Curry [sic] was going to destroy my oath, don't know how long she had been in jail, she came out the day before Commencement [at Brown University], I paid her fine.[15]

It was a standoff. Whether Susan Field had perjured herself three times was never pursued, and although serious doubts had been raised about her testimony, she had managed to testify that the witness against her had been in jail so that Lydia Going's testimony was equally compromised. For the historical record, however, it should be pointed out that Lydia Going's jail sentence was from August 24 to September 3, 1844. Whether Lydia Going really had anything to do with the Brown University commencement, she was not released from jail until afterwards since commencement in those days was on September 1.

Job Wilbur, a prosecution witness in the first Nicholas Gordon trial, had testified that Nicholas had said that "the party had been the means of his not having a license, and he meant to do all he could so [sic] injure the party." This had been placed by the prosecution in the context of Gordon's threats against Sprague. Similarly, Giles James, a prosecution witness in both trials, had testified that Gordon had said in his presence that before another year was out Amasa Sprague, "the damned Algerine," would not be at town council meetings to say whether Gordon would have a license or not.[16] This was taken by the prosecution to be a threat against Sprague's life, to silence him forever. In the second trial, however, the defense made a concerted effort to interpret Nicholas Gordon's threats to mean he intended to get *political* revenge against Sprague.

In accordance with this new defense strategy, in the second trial, Job Wilbur was called as a *defense* witness. In his testimony Wilbur said much the same as he did in the first trial, but this time the thrust of his words was entirely different. Nicholas, he testified, "said he had lost his license because of the *political* party. He meant to injure the party." He added that Nicholas "didn't use the name of Sprague in this connection."[17] In his closing argument, Attorney Rogers emphasized that the evidence indicated that Nicholas Gordon "attributed the loss of his license to political influence" and not to any personal quarrel with Amasa Sprague. "I say," he concluded, "that the Government have most signally failed" to prove Nicholas Gordon's state of mind to be "one of deadly hostility to Amasa Sprague," leading him to incite his brother to murder Sprague.[18]

Conspicuous by its absence in the defense case was any testimony about or even reference to William Gordon's affidavit concerning his concealment of Nicholas's gun and pistol in the attic. The defense team dared not put William on the witness stand for fear that on cross-examination the prosecution might destroy him as a credible witness, and they could not introduce the evidence without first putting William on the stand. Besides, there were too many unanswered questions about why William took so long to make the facts known. The consensus apparently, even among the defense counsel, was that it would be more damaging to Nicholas's case than helpful, particularly since the story seems to have been regarded as a last-minute attempt by the Gordons to save John, rather than the literal truth.

Nonetheless, the defense had to face the fact that the murder weapon had been identified by some prosecution witnesses as the same gun owned by Nicholas. The defense had weakened the prosecution's testimony about the gun upon cross-examination, but now Rogers sought to present witnesses who would testify the murder weapon and Nicholas's gun were not the same. Patrick and Catherine Hawkins (or Harkins) testified about the gun they had seen John Gordon carrying a few days before the murder, which appeared to prove that John not only had access to Nicholas's gun but was seen using it. However, John left the gun with them overnight so that both of them could state positively that John's gun was not the gun produced in court as the murder weapon. Patrick Hawkins described the differences between the two guns and his wife corroborated his description of the differences.[19] Indicative of the lack of thorough preparation of the defense in the John Gordon trial was the fact that Patrick Hawkins was actually called then as a defense witness to testify about the madder dye stains on John's vest and shirt sleeves from the time they worked together at Drybrook, from the end of August to November 1843. Here was an important piece of information because "madder makes a stain like blood," but he was never asked about the gun or shown the murder weapon so that he could point out the differences until this trial, a year later. At the very least it was another missed opportunity in John Gordon's defense at the first trial. Apparently, the defense counsel had not interviewed the Hawkinses about the gun, only about the madder dye. The prosecution was able to raise a doubt as to why now after a year Hawkins was testifying about the gun.

A surprise witness concerning the identification of the gun was none other than Thomas F. Carpenter, who had been on the defense team during the John Gordon trial. His testimony was tantamount to an accusation that William Sprague, brother of Amasa and, until the time of the murder, a United States senator, had bribed a witness to testify for the prosecution:

> Know Benjamin Waterman, the man commonly called Ben Kit. Had some conversation with him during the last trial about his testimony concerning the ramrod [of the murder weapon which was identified by Ben Kit as belonging to Nicholas Gordon]. I was in the office of Walter S. Burges [prominent Providence lawyer and defender of Dorr]. Said he [Ben Kit] was in pursuit of me. Wanted to bring an action against Mr. Sprague. Mr. Sprague had promised him a dollar in money and a jacket. If he would come into Court to testify on this case. I asked him if he had testified. He said he had. Had waited sometime, but Mr. Sprague didn't give him the jacket, and he wanted me to sue him. I told him perhaps he hadn't fulfilled his part of the contract.
>
> He said he had testified as Mr. Sprague wanted him to.[20]

Ben Kit had not been called as a witness in either of the Nicholas Gordon trials, and in that sense "he hadn't fulfilled his part of the contract," but his testimony about the ramrod in the John Gordon trial had been that he was certain it was the one he had ordered made for Nicholas, the same one now on the murder weapon. "I know the ramrod, sir. I should know it in the darkest night ever was seen—tell it by feeling, sir" (*Trial*, 33–34).

William Sprague was called to testify that afternoon:

> Never made any promise to Benjamin Waterman of giving him a dollar, or a jacket, if he would testify here. Did not see him after he was summoned until he appeared in court. He was summoned to the first trial on the suggestion of the prisoners' counsel. I never swoke [sic] to Ben about testifying, or promised or gave him anything.[21]

It was left at that—one man's word against another's. There was no cross-examination and Ben Kit was never called to give his side of the story.

James and Rosannah Stratton testified, as they had in the previous trials, to the fact that they had seen a tall man with a gun near the murder scene shortly before the time of the murder. They had heard the report of a gun from the direction of the murder scene about four o'clock that Sunday afternoon. Chief Justice Durfee intervened at this point and elicited the response from Rosannah that they could not see the murder scene from their house. The Strattons' testimony had seemed a vital piece of evidence during the John Gordon trial, coming as it did at the last minute. It suggested this person, an unknown tall man, much taller than John Gordon so that there could be no mistaking the two, had killed Amasa Sprague. Still, it had not saved John from being convicted. Nonetheless, the defense in its closing argument offered the theory that the tall man was the killer as proof that John was innocent and that therefore Nicholas Gordon was also innocent.

Nicholas Gordon's alleged personal hatred of Amasa Sprague over losing the liquor license was still central to the prosecution's conspiracy theory; consequently, the final witnesses for the defense stressed the alternate view that Gordon's intended revenge was political in nature, not homicidal. William Case testified that Nicholas "said he would have revenge next election, next town meeting," and Andrew Briggs testified that he had actually changed his vote from one party to the other in 1843 because Nicholas had persuaded him that he would not obtain his liquor license if the party he usually voted for succeeded. Finally, the second member of the original defense counsel in the John Gordon trial, John P. Knowles, testified that Nicholas had come to him seeking legal redress for what he considered slanderous allegations in the remonstrance submitted to the town council but then withdrawn.[22] Attorney Rogers stressed in his closing argument that Nicholas "attributed the loss of his license to political influence, to the unjust imputations of his neighbors, and above all his own countrymen" who had signed the remonstrance. The revenge Gordon sought was legal redress, not criminal violence.[23]

Perhaps because he was from Boston rather than Rhode Island and consequently not in awe of the economic and political power William Sprague wielded in the state, Attorney Rogers directly and forcefully attacked Sprague's influence over the prosecution's case. Speaking directly to the jury, he said:

> when I see him (now absent) sitting day after day, by the side of his prosecuting officer [William H. Potter], advising assisting and directing the prosecution, I feel that there is indeed much that is prejudicial to justice, and liable to impress your minds unfavorably toward my client. It may be right, indeed for him, the brother of the deceased,—loving and beloved brothers, I doubt not they were, to see justice done to the perpetrator of the dreadful crime by which that tie was sundered. But to my mind there is something highly improper in the spectacle presented to us. Not with feelings of revenge, or of just retribution, should the State appear here. Last of all, should the counsel of Government be guided by one whose additional sentiments may lead to an unbecoming personal interest in the issue. If it be, that this brother has come here to throw the weight of his character and influence into the scales of the government—I put it to you, acting under the injunction of the oath you have taken, beware of that influence![24]

He did not dare attack William Sprague further for fear of antagonizing the jury, but it was obvious from the beginning that the Sprague family had had undue influence over the investigation and the prosecution of the case against the Gordons. Rogers did go further, however, in asserting the equality of the law in the face of social inequalities and class differences:

> There may be those among you, who think there is little difference between taking the life of a dog and that of an Irishman. Such a belief is alas, too prevalent. But you are not to act upon it. Our institutions recognize no distinction between man and man. The life of Amasa Sprague is no more precious in the eye of the law, than that of Nicholas S. Gordon.[25]

In his closing argument Attorney General Blake summarized the prosecution's case, but he spent most of his time attacking the defense's case as if he recognized the strength of its position and the weakness of his own. He defended Waterman and De Merrit's measurement of the tracks by attacking the inept measurement John O'Brien had made and testified to in the John Gordon trial (but not in this trial). Blake asserted that "the witnesses De Merrit and Waterman are as credible, and as honest as any that can be found in the community," glossing over the fact that they had botched the investigation of the tracks, had ignored other tracks, and had allowed onlookers to mill around, trampling the ground into a confusion of tracks. He defended the testimony of Susan Field by attacking the Gowans [Goings]: "Mr. and Mrs. Gowan have been brought in here to injure her testimony. Such intelligence, such purity, cannot be suspected! Such virtuous, such substantial witnesses, surely must be believed! It is absurd to talk of impeaching her testimony by characters like these."[26] The possibility that Susan Field had perjured herself was dismissed by the attorney general as a joke, rather than as a serious charge to be investigated.

Blake defended the presence of William Sprague at the trial (he had been present at the other two trials as well) as an act stemming from regard for his brother's memory, not from unworthy motives of influence: "It is right that Wm. [William] Sprague should be here. Inhuman and unnatural were it in him not to seek the punishment of his brother's murderers." Finally, he returned to the fateful question that had plagued the Gordons in every trial: Why hadn't Nicholas Gordon produced the coat and the gun said to belong to him if they are not the same ones found at the murder scene? Knowing full well about William Gordon's affidavit, Blake said, "let them but be produced, and he would go free." Blake taunted the defense with the fact that they have not been produced after all this time: "well may the suspicion of guilt fasten upon him, if no attempt is made to produce them."[27] William's last minute attempt to save his brother John from execution had been to no avail. His "confession" was not even used, and the defense's unwillingness to use it became a matter of scornful challenge by the prosecution. There were few in the courtroom and in the jury box who would not understand the taunt.

At 10:30 A.M. on April 17, 1845, the jury foreman informed the court that the jurors were unable to agree on a verdict. Nine were for acquittal, three for conviction. It is unknown why the three jurors voted for conviction. One cannot entirely rule out the possibility that ethnic prejudice played a part in their holding out for conviction. The probable reason for their voting for conviction, and one most likely to ease their consciences, was the unassailable fact that John Gordon had been convicted of murder and executed after the failure of his various appeals. To vote for acquittal was to admit to themselves that there had been a miscarriage of justice, that John Gordon had been innocent as well, which was what nine of their colleagues were in effect admitting. The nine who voted acquittal would have had before them first and foremost the weakness of the case against Nicholas Gordon and the strength of his defense, but undoubtedly behind their verdict was a serious doubt that John Gordon had been guilty of murder. They could do nothing to undo that verdict or John Gordon's execution, but they could and did prevent a repetition of an injustice.

Whatever the factors that went into the individual decisions among the nine jurors, the inescapable conclusion of their vote in the aggregate is that they believed a miscarriage of justice had occurred. The prosecution's case against John Gordon rested on the conspiracy theory, Nicholas Gordon's conspiracy, "with malice aforethought" to incite his brothers to do murder. With William acquitted and the case against Nicholas in grave doubt, the case against John Gordon must have seemed even more uncertain, for even the prosecution never suggested John acted on his own to murder a man he hadn't known existed six months before. At the very least, a reasonable doubt now existed that there had been any conspiracy among the Gordon brothers.

Despite the three to one majority for acquittal, Attorney General Blake opposed bail in any shape or form for Nicholas Gordon. Blake was suspicious that the Gordons and their defense counsel were trying to delay the beginning of another trial "until some important witnesses should be out of the way." Did the attorney general fear the defense would spirit Susan Field out of the state by offering to set her up in a house in Boston or New York? Did he fear the Irish community would drive other witnesses out of town? But the prosecution made no motion for a new trial on the grounds that "the term of the Court has nearly expired." It seemed a lame excuse. In contrast, on the same day Nicholas Gordon's second trial began, Charles Jackson, elected governor on the Liberation Party ticket, called for the release of Dorr from prison and the restoration of his rights as a citizen.[28] The political leaders took care of their own, and Dorr was duly released. No matter how maverick and radical a politician

Dorr might have seemed to some Rhode Islanders, including the jury that found him guilty of treason, he was a member of a prominent family and related to those at the center of political and economic power in the state.

Attorney William Potter, to his credit, "declined making any observation on the question" of bail, but neither did he oppose the attorney general in his vindictiveness. The court for once ruled against the prosecution: "after consultation between the members of the Court, Mr. Chief Justice Durfee said that the case having been committed to a jury, and the jury having in both cases disagreed, we think he must be discharged on bail."[29] Bail was set at $10,000, a sizable sum in those days and certainly "sufficient to secure the presence of the prisoner on his trial."

The attorney general did not relent in his righteous opposition and demanded time to determine the financial responsibility of those offering to put up bail for Nicholas Gordon. Since it was a Friday, Nicholas, who had already spent over a year and three months in prison, might have had to stay another three days because of Blake's intransigence. But either cooler heads prevailed or the attorney general was impressed by the list of sureties—"Jeremiah Baggott, L. Devlin, J.B. Henessey, J. Malay, P. Camble, Wm. Mayghm, N. Figerald, C. Hacket, J. Welch."[30] On Friday April 18, 1845, Nicholas Gordon was "set at liberty," to use the words of the reporter for the *Transcript*. But he was not a free man.

Nicholas Gordon died on October 22, 1846, only eighteen months after he had been released on bail from prison. Within three and a half years he had fallen from a position of success as a man of property and some respect within the Irish community to a man of little property and much debt at the time of his death. All the "goods and chattels rights and credits which were of Nicholas S. Gordon of Providence deceased" amounted to $25.98, minus $4.00 owed the appraisers of his estate. The inventoried goods raised only $17.04 at auction. He left behind a pathetic list of goods—one-half barrel of dried apples worth fifty cents; two oil cans, $2.00; one-half barrel of cider, $1.00; four empty barrels, $2.00; one pair scales and weights, $1.00; a lot of old boxes, $1.00. There were two empty oil barrels, behind which no gun was hidden, worth $1.40. There was one old wagon with no stones in it worth $4.00. The house that also served as a store on leased land in the heart of what is now downtown Providence, was appraised at $733.00, but it was mortgaged to the hilt, $732.80 to be exact, so that his equity in it was twenty cents. He still owned the house/

store in Cranston at the time of his death, but it was only a dwelling place by then, not a place of business. His mother purchased it for $1.00 by decree of the municipal court on July 25, 1848. He left behind him debts totaling $1,322.65.[31]

Within the context of his own ambitions as a small businessman and tavern keeper, Nicholas Gordon had become a success by the spring of 1843. He had achieved the American dream within the limits of his own vision: the oldest son of four, he had come to America in the mid-1830s to seek his fortune, and by the summer of 1843 he had been able to pay the passage of his widowed mother, his sister, his three brothers, and his niece, and had brought them to live with him in Spraguesville or found work and lodging for them in Providence. His sending for them was the apex of his success, but their arrival also coincided with the events leading to his downfall.

It was fateful for the rest of the family, too, and for John and William in particular, that Amasa Sprague was murdered six months after their arrival. Undoubtedly, Nicholas would have been under suspicion anyway because of the quarrel over the liquor license, but the recent arrival of Nicholas's brothers made possible the prosecution's theory that Nicholas had sent for his brothers with murder in his heart, even though that theory does not hold up under examination once the accusation is removed from the hysteria of the anti-Irish, anti-Catholic feeling of the time. In the end, the prosecution's case against Nicholas Gordon faltered on the very point of conspiracy: William as one of the members of the alleged conspiracy was acquitted, and only three jurors were ultimately convinced that Nicholas had incited John to commit murder.

This was no consolation to John Gordon; he was hanged for the murder. He was never to know that his brother Nicholas was not convicted, at least in part exonerating him. John Gordon was the last man ever executed for a crime in Rhode Island. Two other prisoners after him had been sentenced to death by hanging for murder, but one escaped and the other died in prison before he could be executed. It would have been some consolation to John Gordon, perhaps, to know that his death contributed in part to the abolition of capital punishment in Rhode Island which finally occurred in 1852.

The Rhode Island antigallows campaign was part of a national reform movement in the northern states in the antebellum period, but it had only been successful in Michigan, where capital punishment was abolished in

1846. In 1852, after sixteen years of campaigning, the reformers in Rhode Island, led by Thomas Robinson Hazard, finally succeeded in ending capital punishment; life imprisonment replaced the death penalty as the state's severest deterrent.[32] The reformers, however, to gain sufficient support, agreed to retain the death penalty for any person convicted of committing murder while serving a life sentence for any offense, a provision that still exists today in the Rhode Island criminal code.

John Gordon's execution did play some role in the abolition of capital punishment in Rhode Island, although his case was not foremost in the public's mind. On February 11, 1852, shortly before the vote on the issue was taken, Roger Williams Potter, sheriff of Providence County in 1845 and John Gordon's hangman, testified before the state house of representatives:

> that neither he nor his wife had been the same persons they were before [the execution], and that the effects of the shock then given to his nervous system and health still remained with him. The evident truthfulness of the statement of the witness, joined to his modest, dignified demeanor, made a profound impression on the House.[33]

The overwhelming vote to abolish capital punishment, forty-four to twenty, was something of an indication of the serious doubts still prevalent about John Gordon's guilt.

The Gordon family had lived under a cloud ever since that fateful Sunday afternoon, December 31, 1843. Even after he was released from prison on bail, Nicholas Gordon was still under threat of another trial; the charges had not been dismissed, and he was still under indictment for murder. With the help of the Providence Irish community he attempted to make a new start by opening the store in the city. This was the one bright spot in the sad story; for if he blamed the Irish workmen in Spraguesville for losing him the liquor license by signing Sprague's remonstrance from fear of losing their jobs, the Irish in Providence had rallied to his support both during and after the trials. Margaret McCoy had loaned him $500 to help pay for his defense, secured by Gordon's Cranston land. Jeremiah Baggott and John B. Hennessey also supported him financially, but Nicholas could recover neither his money nor his health, and he died a failure, never regaining his right to vote because his property was encumbered by debt.

There would be those at the time who, still believing the Gordons were guilty, could see a moral tale in the downfall of Nicholas Gordon. What then would they make of William Gordon, tailor, found not guilty of any crime, a free man after his trial, but who, having acted out of ignorance and the mistaken belief he was helping his brothers, concealed vital evidence that might have freed them? It might seem poetic justice that on June 18, 1850, Israel V. Potter, deputy sheriff of Providence County arrested William Gordon, "for want of the goods and chattels of the within named William Gordon to be by me found within my precincts, whereon to levy this execution, I have taken the body of the said William and him committed to the State Jail in this County," the same jail from which he had walked out six years earlier, a free man.[34]

The imprisonment of William Gordon, debtor, was in consequence of a judgment against him and his mother by John B. Hennessey, acting on behalf of the estate of the late Margaret McCoy, who in 1845 had loaned Nicholas $500, secured by land in Cranston. For want of $18.54, the cost of the suit, plus twenty-five cents for the writ, William was imprisoned. Although Ellen Gordon was also specifically named in the writ along with William to be taken to the county jail and "therein to be kept until they pay the full sum above mentioned," she was not arrested.

The saddest story of all was Ellen Gordon's. Two of her sons dead, a third in prison, and the fourth disappeared as though he had never existed, she was without visible support. Whether she was ever arrested and put into debtor's prison is unknown, but she was unable to pay the taxes on the house in Spraguesville for 1851, a grand total of $1.20. The house was sold at public auction on January 5, 1852 to Nehemiah R. Knight for $4.75.[35]

The house with its attached store no longer exists, although as late as 1930 it still stood on the northerly side of the road, leading from the factory village of the estate of Amasa Sprague deceased, to Monkey Town (as Knightsville was called) in Cranston. A house of death, someone once called it, and let that be its epitaph. The land on which it stood is now part of a Catholic cemetery.

CHAPTER EIGHT

Who Killed Amasa Sprague?

On July 12, 1845, an irate citizen, signing himself "an Irishman," wrote to the editor of the *Boston Pilot* that the criminal justice system in the United States in general and in Massachusetts and Rhode Island in particular was prejudiced against the Irish. He cited in evidence the fact that Gordon in Rhode Island and Barrett in Massachusetts had been hanged on the basis of circumstantial evidence, whereas within the same year the "American" murderers of three Irishmen had only been given prison sentences, even though the evidence against them was direct. The editor commented that he concurred "heartily and thoroughly with the views of the writer," who demanded equal justice for all and that capital punishment, since it was the law, "be fairly dispensed to all."

From the perspective of nearly a century and a half, it is apparent that John Gordon was a victim of a widespread prejudice against the Irish among the native white Americans in Rhode Island and also a victim of a criminal justice system that made it difficult, if not impossible, for him to receive a fair and impartial trial. His ethnic peers had been largely excluded from juries because naturalized citizens were unable to vote or serve on juries unless they owned real estate valued at $134 and unencumbered by debt. No Irishman served on any of the three juries trying the Gordons. John Gordon's only avenue of judicial appeal was to the same court and the same judges who had presided over his trial and acted at times as though they were the prosecutors. His only appeal of last resort was to a state legislature dominated by conservative political forces and to a conservative governor from the same party who had no pardoning power under the state constitution until 1854. It was not until a half century later that the federal courts considered appeals based on decisions by state courts in criminal cases.

Still, the jury system muddled through. William Gordon was acquitted by the same jury that found his brother John guilty. The jurors were not so blindly prejudiced that they were going to convict William against all the facts of his alibi. He was the victim of an obvious case of mistaken identity, and the jurors rejected the prosecution's weak case against him. Furthermore, John Gordon was not only a victim of a prejudiced criminal justice system but of his own family and friends as well. His mother's damaging pretrial statements and his brother's act of hiding the gun did as much to convict him as the prosecution's case against him. He was a victim of circumstances as well as a victim of circumstantial evidence, and he was a victim of his own folly as well as his brother William's in keeping the fact of the hidden gun from the court and from his own defense counsel.

But if the Gordons, John, William, and Nicholas, were innocent, who then murdered Amasa Sprague? The controversy surrounding the guilt or innocence of the Gordon brothers—Nicholas's two trials ending in hung juries extended the controversy beyond John's execution—obscured this question for a long time. The identity of the tall man and the short man seen by Barker and Spencer remained a mystery, as did the identity of the man seen by Stratton and others stalking Amasa. To offer these men as the murderers merely begs the question of who did the killing. The secret of who murdered Amasa Sprague is locked in the community itself. This was not a casual killing or an unpremeditated act of violence. Sunday, late in the afternoon, was chosen because no one would question the fact that the murderers were carrying guns at a time when others in the village might also be hunting small game. It was known Amasa Sprague walked along the driftway to his farm on Sunday afternoons. The killing had to take place near sunset in the hope the body would remain undetected until the next day, but not after dark, for who would be hunting then? A shot that late in the day might be investigated. But the shot only disabled Amasa, not killing him outright. Amasa struggled, and he was beaten to death.

After 150 years it is of course impossible to prove who killed Amasa Sprague. There were no deathbed confessions by the Gordons or anyone else. Still, after all this time there exists a tantalizing urge to "solve" the murder, particularly because the miscarriage of justice that followed leaves the question of who did it unanswered. We offer a hypothetical theory for the identity of a possible murderer, an accessory before the fact, if not for the identity of the immediate assailants. We present it as an entirely speculative hypothesis since it is wholly circumstantial, but then so also was much of the testimony against Nicholas Gordon. Our conjecture is that the man who might have plotted the murder of Amasa Sprague was his brother William, and that William Sprague could have conspired to incite and hire others to murder his brother while he was safely in Washington with an ironclad alibi. While there is no direct evidence against William Sprague, not even an open public quarrel between the two brothers, nonetheless William Sprague stood to benefit most from Amasa's death. Any investigation into the murder should have included him as a suspect, especially since the case rested on a theory of conspiracy in which the primary instigator provided himself with an unassailable alibi.

William was odd man out in the partnership of the A. & W. Sprague Company. Amasa was firmly entrenched in Spraguesville, living in the homestead and running the main factory of the company, the Cranston Print Works. Their brother-in-law Emanuel Rice was running the cotton mills in Natick that fed cloth to the print works. Amasa liked this arrangement, which worked and was profitable. But he opposed any further expansion of the business. In earlier years, while his father was still alive, William had run the Natick mills, tinkered with machinery, and acted as agent selling the manufactured cloth and calico prints to markets outside the state. But even at that time he was not as involved as Amasa in the actual operation of the business. After the father's death in 1836 Amasa became the senior partner in the firm and took control. William went into politics as a career and was successful, but politics seemed neither to satisfy him personally nor to absorb his energies. Elected to the U.S. House of Representatives in 1836, he made no speeches and was absent most of the time, attending to the settlement of his father's estate in Rhode Island. He was elected governor by a narrow majority in 1838 but was defeated the next year, the term of governor being then only for one year. His appointment to the U.S. Senate by the Rhode Island legislature early in 1842 should have been the crowning achievement of his political career, but the machinations of local politics seemed to intrigue him more than national issues. Although he had been elected senator with the help of the Dorrites, he became personally involved in using his influence in the state to defeat the suffrage movement under Dorr. He and Amasa opposed Dorr because their own power and influence in Cranston and

William Sprague (1799–1856).
From *Providence Sunday Journal*, October 2, 1932.

the state depended on the status quo of the old established order. Their brother-in-law Emanuel Rice openly bought votes against the Dorr constitution which would have liberalized voting qualifications and changed the balance of power in the state.[1]

William's lack of political principle and his love of political intrigue were consistent with the rest of his personality. He was a secretive man, reticent, seldom showing his emotions, whereas Amasa tended to flare up emotionally when provoked. William kept himself to himself. His brooding temperament made him look gloomy, and his large body accentuated his personal aura of isolation.[2] Unscrupulous, shrewd, and practical, as well as autocratic and feudalistic, he was better suited to the nineteenth-century politics of business than to the business of politics.[3] But Amasa was in the way; he wouldn't budge; he wouldn't expand the business; he had no vision. One thing that national politics had done for William was to free him from parochial limitations and give him a broader view. He wanted to use the company's profits to expand; Amasa wanted to save the profits for his family and keep the status quo. Amasa was only forty-five in 1843; he had at least twenty more years ahead of him as the senior partner of the firm, at a time when the country was crying out for expansion. Textile manufacturers all over New England were expanding to share in the prosperity. The Panic of 1837 was behind them, but Amasa was acting as though it was still going on.

In this speculative theory of who killed Amasa Sprague, William Sprague would stand in the same relationship to the crime under the law as Nicholas Gordon had been—an accessory before the fact—and he would be as guilty of murder as those who actually did the killing. The essential difference, however, is that William made no public threats against Amasa as Nicholas had done. William Sprague, home for the summer recess, would have been well aware of the quarrel between Amasa and Nicholas over the renewal of the license; indeed, Amasa himself told William that Nicholas Gordon had made threats against him.[4] This could possibly have given William the idea of diverting suspicion from himself, who would benefit from Amasa's death, to an Irishman who had made threats in public and vowed to get even with Amasa. He would know, to use prosecution attorney William Potter's words at the trial, that "a conspiracy need not be proved by the declarations of the persons forming it. It may be proved by the *acts* of the persons engaged in it." The act of murder would immediately throw suspicion on Nicholas Gordon, not on William Sprague. He would hurry back from Washington to take charge of the investigation and thus make sure the Gordons were indicted and convicted for murder.

Brotherly love is a romantic ideal; Cain and Abel a biblical story. Both are deeply embedded in the mythology and literature of our culture. Sibling rivalry can be a motivating factor in human behavior; so also is fraternal loyalty. The attorney general made much of the mystique of kinship, describing it as a special characteristic of the Irish: "The Irish have strong propensities; strong attachments and resentments; qualities which, under a favorable development, tend to ennoble, but under an unfavorable one, to debase the mind. One of the strongest and most marked features of the Irish character . . . is the strength of their national and fraternal feeling. The tie of kindred is to an Irishman almost an indissoluble bond" (*Trial*, 132).

On the basis of this mystique of kinship, we are expected to believe that John and William Gordon so debased their minds with hate and revenge, within six months of arriving in this country, that they committed murder on their brother Nicholas's say so, unquestioningly and out of blind loyalty to him. It would be no more fanciful to suggest that William Sprague, out of a sibling rivalry that had turned to suppressed hatred, convinced himself that his brother Amasa had to be done away with for the good of the family, for the best interests of the company, even for the prosperity of the nation itself, which depended on the continuing expansion of industry by energetic, visionary entrepreneurs like himself and his father. From that distorted perspective, Amasa was an obstacle that had to be removed.

Once William Sprague took over the Sprague Company, he was in complete control. Amasa's two sons, Amasa and William, were minors, and their uncle became their legal guardian, controlling their share of the enterprise. The widow deferred to him in financial matters, and the older son, Amasa, who was fifteen, was placed in the firm's accounting office in Providence to learn the business. His younger brother, William, eventually went into politics, the careers of the two brothers replicating those of the older generation.

The "remarkable and beautiful instance of fraternal affection" between Amasa and William Sprague that Attorney General Blake had praised in the John Gordon trial became by the second Nicholas Gordon trial almost as mystical a fraternal bond as the one that supposedly existed among the Gordon brothers. "Through life," Blake rhapsodized, "they were one and inseparable, united in heart and in fortune, a most remarkable instance of fraternal affection."[5] There is no question that Amasa and William were united in fortune; the company was a partnership in which neither brother could act without the other's consent. But as far as their personal, as opposed to their business, relationship were concerned, each had gone his own way and pursued his own career. They did not live in the same county, let alone the same township; their lives were separate except for their joint ownership of the business itself. Blake's claim that they were "united in heart" may have been nothing more than a conventional platitude. Whatever William's true feelings, he kept his emotions under control.

It would behoove William to hide his feelings if the idea of getting rid of Amasa transformed itself from wish to plan. Perhaps he had tried once more to convince Amasa to go along with him to expand the business. Perhaps his plan was only to disable Amasa so that he could take over control of the company, but the hired thugs botched the job and had to make sure that Amasa was dead. Perhaps Amasa was to have been ambushed and quickly killed with a single shot. In any case William would have to be sure that he was in Washington at the time and not still home for the Christmas recess.

One can almost hear Attorney General Blake ask a witness, a visitor in Washington at the time of the murder, as he asked John DeFoster, resident of Cranston visiting in Providence, the day of the murder: "Did you see Nicholas S. Gordon/William Sprague in town that day? If so, when and where." And William Sprague's defense attorney, surely not Samuel Atwell, would also object to the question. The attorney general would then in all seriousness state, as he did in the first trial, "we propose to prove that Nicholas S. Gordon/William Sprague was in town during the day of the murder, and consequently could not have committed it." All involved in the proceedings would know said Gordon/Sprague had an alibi and that the purpose of the questioning was to suggest that the alibi was deliberately planned as part of the conspiracy. In either case the fact that Gordon/Sprague was in town would not be contested by the defense.

Once back in Rhode Island, William Sprague controlled the investigation. He offered the $1,000 reward in the name of the family. As coordinator of the information being gathered by the vigilance committees he knew how the investigation was progressing and was able to focus on the Gordons as the suspects. He could suppress information and testimony that tended to show the involvement of suspects other than the Gordons. James Stratton came to him with the evidence that he had seen a man with a gun stalking Amasa Sprague shortly before the murder, but Sprague did not pass the information to the prosecution, claiming that Stratton

141

changed his story later. Charles Searle, who had overheard the conversation, knew when to keep his mouth shut and claimed he never mentioned the conversation because no one had asked him about it.

Stratton's testimony about the man with a gun was corroborated by his next-door neighbor, Francis M'Clocklin, as well as by his wife. It was vital information that should have been pursued with the same vigor with which clues pointing to John Gordon were investigated, but the lead was never followed. True, Francis M'Clocklin (or McLaughlin) was interviewed by Rollin Mathewson and his testimony taken down, but Mathewson was William Sprague's nephew and his instructions would have been clear—concentrate on the Gordons. M'Clocklin's testimony that the man with the gun was "taller than either of the prisoners," would have undermined the prosecution's case against the Gordons. The investigators led by William Sprague were interested in convicting the Gordons, not in discovering the truth. To safeguard against testimony by Stratton and others, the prosecution included in the indictment "some person unknown" as a co-conspirator.

The fact that this man, a tall stranger with a gun, was seen in the vicinity of the murder just fifteen minutes before witnesses heard the report of a gunshot, strongly suggests he was one of the murderers. But he was definitely not one of the Gordons. The two men seen by Barker and Spencer both shortly before and after the murder with one gun between them were also probably involved in the murder of Amasa Sprague, but the shorter man of the two was definitely not William Gordon. They were three strangers with at least two guns between them, and they knew the terrain well enough to stalk Amasa from different directions, entrap him, and ambush him. They were hunting, but their prey was a human being. Defense Attorney Thomas Carpenter had argued that the two men seen together were the assassins: "These men were no doubt the murderers of Amasa Sprague." Defense Attorney Samuel Atwell was equally convinced that the man seen by the Strattons and M'Clocklin was the murderer. It is our theory that all three were stalking Amasa Sprague and encircling him, the two waiting in ambush near the foot bridge on the Johnston side, the third following behind Amasa on the Cranston side. There were people about and it was risky, but they had the best disguise possible—they were assumed to be hunters. It explained the gun; it explained their presence in the immediate area; it explained their stalking the "game."

The assassins were lucky—even though they were seen twice by two witnesses, the shorter of the two was mistakenly identified by both witnesses as being William Gordon. It was a stroke of luck for William Sprague, if he was the one who hired these three men to kill his brother, that William Gordon hid his brother Nicholas's gun, making the case against the Gordons so much easier for the prosecution.

To make sure his interests were being served by the prosecution during the trials, William Sprague hired a bright young lawyer in the former attorney general's law office, William H. Potter, to assist the new attorney general. The new attorney general could be relied on to prosecute the Gordons vigorously, but Sprague wanted a ready excuse to consult with the prosecution about the progress of the case. Not satisfied with secondhand reports about the trials, he attended the court sessions himself so that he could know firsthand how the trial was developing. More important, he could sit next to William Potter and consult and advise him about the proceedings. Even during Nicholas Gordon's second trial, the third against the Gordons, he sat in the courtroom listening to the witnesses, hearing again for the third time the gory details of his brother's murder. By then John Gordon had already been executed for the murder. But Sprague would not be satisfied until Nicholas Gordon himself was found guilty. Until that happened there was always the chance that the whole fabric of the case against the Gordons would unravel, and the authorities would have to look elsewhere for the murderers. William Gordon had been acquitted, and just before John Gordon's execution William's affidavit claiming he hid the gun was publicly circulated. John Gordon in death was seen as a martyr by some, and serious questions were being raised about his guilt. Nicholas Gordon was not yet convicted, and if he were acquitted in this trial, who would believe John Gordon had been guilty on his own?

It must have galled William Sprague to be compelled to take the witness stand in his own defense against the accusation of attempting to bribe a witness, Benjamin Waterman, better known as Ben Kit, the village fool. It was his word against Ben Kit's, but it was a measure of the changing political times that he had to defend himself at all. His presence throughout the trial and his rebuttal testimony elicited direct criticism from defense attorney Rogers in his closing statement, who saw this as an attempt "to throw the weight of his character and influence into the scale of the government" and thus to unduly influence the jury's verdict.

No jury would have convicted William Sprague on the basis of the hypothetical "evidence" speculated upon here, anymore than the actual jury in the first trial convicted William Gordon on the basis of mistaken identity. Still, the prosecution indicted William Gordon and brought him to trial, no matter how weak the case against him. Justice required that William Sprague, who had the most to gain financially from the murder of his brother, at least be investigated instead of being allowed, as he was, to direct and control the investigation and to hire his own prosecutor to pursue the case in court against the Gordons.

Only after Nicholas Gordon's death did William Sprague begin to lay the foundation for the Sprague industrial empire, the realization of his dream of an ever-expanding business. In 1848 he built a stone cotton mill at Coventry, Rhode Island, some 350 feet long, 55 feet wide and four stories high, eventually housing 500 looms. A short distance down river he built another mill with about half the capacity of the first. A whole new village, Quidnic, was created. In 1853, he constructed his largest mill to date, operating over 600 looms. He built a permanent dam to provide the power for the looms and a village of double tenement houses for his workers. He called it Arctic. All this expansion was coordinated with the expansion of the Cranston Print Works for the printing of calico cloth.[6]

His ambitions did not stop there, now that there was no obstacle to his dream of empire building. He was instrumental in the financing of the Hartford, Providence and Fishkill Railroad, making sure that the tracks ran close to the print works in Spraguesville and all the cotton mills that fed the print works. To finance these enterprises he obtained controlling interest in the Globe Bank and the Bank of Commerce in Providence. But it was the building of mills and mill villages that excited him the most and stimulated his imagination. He went beyond the boundaries of the state to build new mills in nearby Connecticut. His dream was to build the largest cotton mill in New England. The main building was to be 644 feet long and 68 feet wide, with wings that would make it 954 feet long in all. It would be the culmination of his career. He called the mill and its satellite village Baltic. Eventually the township in which it was located was named Sprague in his honor.[7]

The building of the mill commenced, but only the foundation had been dug when William Sprague died of typhoid fever in October 1856, almost ten years after the death of Nicholas Gordon. They were all dead then (if William Gordon was still alive he was gone from the state, living else-where, perhaps under an assumed name), the brothers whose lives had

Textile label from A. & W. Sprague, showing the Spraguesville Mill, 1850

been inextricably woven together in death. The younger generation took over and expanded the business even more.[8] But the foundation William Sprague left behind at his death was symbol enough.

What he loved most was to design and build mills. As Mathias P. Harpin wrote in *The High Road to Zion*, "he confided to friends that he was happiest when building a new mill."[9] It must have been with a mixture of pride and joy that he watched the foundation being dug. The Baltic mill alone would operate nearly 2,000 looms with 32,000 spindles feeding the looms and employing 1,200 hands. The Cranston Print Works was producing at the same time 40,000 pieces of calico cloth per week, employing 500 operatives, the total population of Spraguesville in Amasa's time. It soon became the largest calico printing company in the world. And he,

William Sprague, had set the foundation. But the foundation, if our theory is correct, was built on the moral quicksand of fratricide. It would be too much to say that the collapse of the Sprague empire in bankruptcy in 1873 was caused by the murder of Amasa Sprague, but inevitably, inexorably, the ever-expanding production of cloth and the ever-increasing profits were heading for disaster.

At the beginning of 1873 the Sprague mills produced more calico cloth than all the other factories in the United States combined; their output represented one-fourth of all the spindles operating in the country; their profits had reached $20,000,000 and the firm itself was worth a half-billion dollars. But by the end of the year the company was bankrupt. The forces of overproduction that William Sprague unleashed in 1844 led to that moment of complete shutdown, the machinery idle, the operatives thrown out of work, the mills eventually sold at great loss to B. B. and R. Knight Company and others. It was the end of the Sprague Company, the death of an American empire, the largest business failure in American industrial history at the time.[10]

APPENDIX

Petition and Affidavits, February 1845

Providence Feb. 10, 1845
12½ o'clock

Hon. James Fenner

Sir—

A friend has within the hour informed me that he has good reason to believe that the Judges of the Supreme Court are unanimously of opinion that John Gordon ought, as a matter of right, to be reprieved, until after a second trial of his brother Nicholas:— for on his trial, Nicholas assumes on himself the burthen of proving the innocence of John. He assumed this on his late trial, and as a Juror, Mr Mathewson, informs me, the Jury disagreed upon John's case, rather than upon that of Nicholas.

The same friend also informs me that he has reason to believe that the Court hold that under the 4th Section of Article 7 of the Constitution, the Executive may reprieve, notwithstanding that a Session of the Assembly has intervened between the day of sentence and the date of the application for a reprieve. I take the liberty to mention this, because the petititon of Gordon which I drew, evinces a doubt on this point in the mind of the writer. I frankly grant that I had a doubt in regard to the construction of the law of the Section.

Craving pardon for troubling you with this note

I am with great respect,

Your Excellency's obedient servant

John P. Knowles
Atty of John Gordon

APPENDIX

John Gordon's Petition

To His Excellency JAMES FENNER, *Governor of the State of Rhode Island*

The undersigned, John Gordon, a convict under sentence of death, humbly asks from your Excellency an examination of the accompanying affidavits; and in view of their contents, and of the circumstances under which he was convicted, (too familar to all to be here recited,) invokes such action on your part as to your Excellency shall seem meet.

He is sentenced to be executed on Friday next, the 14th instant, between the hours of nine and three. The facts set forth in the affidavit of William Gordon, considered in connexion with the testimony upon which your petitioner was convicted—facts withheld by the petitioner, even from his counsel, lest by a disclosure he should jeopard his brother William, and never divulged to Counsel until Saturday last—these facts, your petitioner submits, entitle him to ask a reprieve until his brother Nicholas shall have been again tried.

Wherefore he would now, as a citizen preferring a not unreasonable petition to the Executive Power, ask from your Excellency, (if constitutionally it may be,) a reprieve "until the end of the next session of the Assembly;" or such other proper executive action, as shall afford him an opportunity to solicit from the Legislature of the State a consideration of his case, and that reprieve, which recently (for want of that which is herewith presented,) was denied him.

And as in duty bound, will pray.

(Signed,)   JOHN GORDON

I, WILLIAM GORDON, of Providence, in the county of Providence, declare and say, That the first information I received of the murder of the late Mr. Amasa Sprague, was from a shoemaker whose shop was in the building next the house in which I boarded at the time. I called at his shop on the morning after the murder and he mentioned the circumstances as the news of the morning. I told him I could not believe the story, for I was out at Cranston the afternoon before, and heard nothing about it. He replied that he had seen the newspaper which contained an account of the matter, and he believed it. I then went to my work at Mr. O'Brien's tailor's shop, where the murder was several times the subject of conversation among the visitors, and inmates of the shop, I taking part in the conversation, and continuing to express my doubts as to the truth of the reports. About noon, however, my brother Nicholas with a man, a stranger to me, came to the shop, and from him we learned that there was no doubt of the death of Mr. Sprague. O'Brien was in the shop all the time Nicholas stayed, and one or two other persons, whose names I cannot now recall. Nicholas wished me to come out to Cranston and spend New Year's Day, with my family, saying it was the first New Year's Day that had come since John and I had arrived in America, and it was too bad I should work that day. I was willing, and rather wished to go, but my employer, Mr. O'Brien objected, as he needed my work that day; but said I might go in the evening. I continued working until towards dusk, when I set off on foot for Cranston. On arriving near the house of Mr. Sprague, I noticed quite a body of men coming down the road, who turned off into Mr. Sprague's house, when I was within thirty or forty rods of them. This excited my curiosity, and when, on arriving near the bridge in the hollow, I met two men, I spoke to them, bidding them "good evening," intending to enquire of them what was the occasion of the gathering of the people which I had witnessed a few moments before. These men proved to be William Tately and William Downey, with both of whom I was acquainted, and one of whom, on my saying "good evening," recognised me and replied "William is that you?" In reply to my question as to the cause of the assemblage just now referred to, they told me that my brothers Nicholas and John had been arrested for the murder of Mr. Sprague, and were in the crowd I had seen. After a few minutes' conversation in the road, Downey proposed to Tately to turn about and accompany me to my mother's, and Tately somewhat reluctantly consented, and we all proceeded to the house. We found there was no one but my mother and my little daughter. My mother was weeping, but was able to converse. I proposed to go down to Mr. Sprague's to see my brothers, but was told by Tately and Downey that it would do no good, as probably they had been carried directly to Providence. Tately and Downey, after a few minutes left the house, myself, my mother, and the little girl remaining. For several minutes I paced the room, my mother and the girl being seated at the fire, but at length I took the lamp from the mantle piece, and without any motive or purpose that I can now recollect, left the room, (the kitchen) and passing into the room connecting the kitchen with the shop, tried to open the door of the shop. It proved to be fastened on the shop side, and I could not open it. I then turned and opened the door of the room on the right hand of the room in which I was, and on entering saw Nicholas's gun standing in the corner of the room on the right of the door.

It instantly occurred to me that as John and Nicholas had been arrested, the house would be searched to find weapons, and that as in my own country, where few persons, comparatively, of the poorer classes possess arms, the finding of weapons in the house of the suspected is almost enough to insure a conviction, it would be greatly to my brothers' advantage to conceal the gun. I then, according to the best of my recollection, instantly returned to the kitchen door which I had left partly open, and closed it; and then taking the gun went up-stairs with it into the garret. Then turning to the left, I tore up the cloth carpeting between the two beds which stood there, and tried to loosen one of the floor boards with my fingers. Failing in this, I looked around for some implement to aid me, and after a few minutes' search found a crooked piece of iron, with which I forced up the end of one of the floor boards and thrust the gun in as far as it would go. The gun was not yet wholly out of sight, and I therefore attempted to raise the next board. In doing this I split the board, but accomplished my purpose, as I was then able to put the gun out of sight. I then replaced the boards, settling the nails in their places with my boot heel, and tacked down the carpeting over them, leaving the floor in appearance the same as I found it.—My impression is, that after reaching the garret, I ascertained by the ramrod, that the gun was loaded; but I cannot say that I recollect doing so. After this, I returned to the kitchen where my mother and daughter still were, and there remained until nine or ten o'clock, when we all retired to rest. Nothing was said by me to her about the gun, nor by her to me. I have no reason to believe, nor do I believe, that she either knew or suspected that there was a gun in the house at the time.

The next morning, about eight o'clock, on going to the kitchen closet for some purpose not now recollected, I found lying upon the upper shelf a small pocket pistol, which I knew to be Nicholas', as I had often seen it in his possession. This I immediately took up, and for the same reason which had actuated me in conceal-ing the gun, proceeded forthwith to secrete. I went up stairs with it, and on looking round for a fit hiding place, noticed the hole in the floor through which the stove pipe from the shop passed. I perceived that between the joists under the garret floor was a cavity, and into that I put the pistol, pushing it in as far as I could with a stick about a yard long. I said nothing to my mother or any one else at the time about the pistol.

About nine or ten o'clock the same morning, (Tuesday) I started from home for the Jail, to see my brothers, intending to acquaint them with my proceedings in relation to the gun and pistol; but on reaching the Jail was denied access to them, and thereupon set off for home. On the road home, and when within about a hundred yards of Mr. Sprague's house, I was met by the Sheriff and his posse, who arrested me and committed me to Jail. There I was kept secluded from communi-cation from any one but the officers of the prison for eight or nine days, when Mr. Knowles was permitted to see me, preparatory to the examination which was to be had the next day. My brothers I did not see until I met them in the Jailer's office in presence of the examining magistrate; and there I once attempted to speak with Nicholas, to inform him of the facts above stated, but was checked by the officers in attendance, and constrained to remove to a distance from him.

I cannot now recollect when I communicated these facts to my brothers John and Nicholas. I do not recollect that I ever stated them to Nicholas. Until I had been tried and discharged, I never had the opportunity to converse with him. To John I communicated them while our trial was in progress in the Court room. Neither John nor I communicated them to the counsel in the case. I dared not disclose them, for I felt assured that they would be regarded as evidence of my guilt; and John refrained from disclosing them because he thought with me, that to disclose them would ensure my conviction. He was, however, not unmindful that the production of the gun and pistol might have saved him from conviction; and when the verdict of guilty was rendered against him, he spoke, as I believe, his honest opinion when he said to me as he resumed his seat, "it is you, William, that have hung me."—a remark so well warranted by the facts, and so accordant with my own views at the moment, that it deprived me for many minutes of all self-control, and reduced me, as all present will recollect, for a time, to a state of infantile helplessness, both intellectually and physically.

I had, previous to being put upon trial, hoped and believed that Nicholas would be first tried and in that case intended to divulge these facts; and with reference to this, had on all occasions urged the counsel of Nicholas to arrange that he be tried first, telling him in general terms that I could put Nicholas in possession of facts that would clear him. But it was so ordered, that I was first tried with my brother John; and up to the termination of that trial, to no person but to John had I ever communicated my knowledge respecting the gun and the pistol.

I was acquitted, but my brother was found guilty. My brother impressed with the belief, and I sharing it, that had I disclosed the facts known to me, he would have been acquited also. I wonder not that weeks and months afterwards my conduct and deportment were such as led my counsel and my friends to lend but an inattentive ear to my communications; to regard me, as some did, as a man of disordered intellect. My conscience was burthened; not with any secret connected with the murder of Mr. Sprague, for of that dark deed I know nothing; but with the secret, that evidence which, as I view the case, might have saved a beloved brother from the gallows, had been by me selfishly suppressed, even while that more generous brother sat beside me acquainted with the same facts, yet, for my sake, withholding them. That I was at times almost frantic I find no difficulty in believing.

A few days after my acquittal, availing myself of the temporary absence from home of my mother and sister, I took the gun from its hiding place and drew the charge. It was loaded with powder and shot. I then put it back in the cavity, and there it remained undisturbed, until last fall, when I exhibited it to a Mr. Mathewson and a Mr. Chapman, as will appear hereafter. Shortly after this I drew the pistol out of the place where I had put it, and laid it in Nicholas' trunk down stairs, where it remained unseen so far as I know, until within a few days, when I showed it to Mr. John Devlin, of Pawtucket.

I cannot say that I ever stated to any of the counsel of myself or my brothers, that I knew aught of the gun or pistol. My belief is that I never did to any of them, excepting Mr. Rogers, say that I knew where Nicholas' gun was. I had, however, up to a very recent period, a full belief that the facts were known, both to Mr.

APPENDIX

Curry [*sic*] and to General Carpenter; and therefore, when a few days before Nicholas' trial I was asked by Mr. Rogers if I knew where Nicholas' gun was, I told him I did, and added "Mr. Carpenter will tell you whole,"—I not doubting that I should be called on when the Court sat to produce the gun and pistol, and testify in regard to them. Under this impression I attended the Court from day to day expecting to be called. But unfortunately it so happened that when I was called (as I am informed I was) I was absent; and the counsel, it appears, did not deem my testimony of sufficient importance to send for me, or to call me, the next day. It seems that they knew not that I could give any information about the gun or pistol—that I had been in error in supposing them advised of my knowledge. My brother's case went to the jury; my testimony not before them. Fortunately for my future peace that jury did not convict. But there was still occasion for the deepest sorrow and regret. Upon the trial of Nicholas I had been led to believe depended in some degree the fate of John. Could Nicholas have been acquitted, John might escape the gallows. But Nicholas not acquitted, would John be reprieved? Again I was almost wild with anguish and despair.

On the day of the dismissal of the Jury by which Nicholas was tried, while riding on the Johnston road with two acquaintances, we overtook two men on foot, one of whom I recognized as one of the Jury. We entered into a conversation which continued until we arrived near Dyer's Bridge, when the man above referred to (whom I have since learned is named Mathewson) requested some one of us acquainted with the ground to accompany him and his companion over it, to point out the several localities referred to on the late trial. I offered to accompany them, and accordingly went with them over the fields to the spot of the murder, and on the driftway over Hawkins' Hole. Mr. Mathewson, shortly after crossing the bridge at Hawkins's Hole, expressed his opinion that John could not have committed the murder; but added, that he did think Nicholas must have known something about it. In the course of his remarks, he said in effect, that the gun with which the murder was committed, was Nicholas' gun. This remark brought freshly to my recollection, my own position with regard to the gun and pistol, and my anguish of heart sought relief in tears. I however retained sufficient self-command to say to him that the gun found and produced in court was not Nicholas' gun. This declaration seemed to arouse him, and he, with some warmth, proceeded to recapitulate the evidence given at the trial in regard to the ownership of the gun: asking in conclusion, and in a triumphant tone, "if the gun produced in court was not Nicholas' gun, where is the gun which he owned to Dr. Cleveland he bought at Almy's?"

Under the influence of sorrow and remorse, I answered him that I knew where it was, and could show it to him if he would go to the house. He and his companion at once agreed to go, and to the house we went. I took the gentlemen up stairs, and, removing the carpet and lifting the board, drew from its hiding place the gun, a half-stocked gun, with percussion lock, iron trimmings, and a small bore, the only gun of that description which, to my knowledge, my brother Nicholas ever possessed. He had formerly a musket gun, which he gave to a Mrs. Mulloy, on her departure for the west; but of fowling guns, with percussion lock, I never saw any other than this in my brother's hands or house. In reply to the questions of Mr. Mathewson, I stated why I secreted the gun, and when; and why I did not divulge the facts on my trial. I offered also to show Mr. Mathewson the pistol which was below stairs; but I understood him to say—"no matter about it," or something to that effect. I believe I requested Mr. Mathewson to keep my communication secret. Mr. Mathewson told me that my testimony would be very important to Nicholas in his next trial, said that I must not fail then to appear with the gun and the pistol. This advice coincided with my own views, and I determined to say nothing more about the matter until Nicholas should be again tried. I was induced to believe by what I heard from my friends and acquaintances, that John would be reprieved by the Legislature until after Nicholas should be again tried; and therefore still trusted that I should be able by stating the facts within my knowledge, to save the life of my brother John. But the Legislature denied to John the reprieve he asked, and again I became the prey of remorse.

Although since my conversation with Mr. Mathewson, (who laughed at my fears and assured me that I could not again be arrested and tried,) I had not, as was previously the case, been deterred from speaking freely, by a dread of bringing upon myself another prosecution, I do not recollect that I again mentioned the fact of my having the gun to any one, until last Thursday. On that day, being at work in the shop with my employer, Patrick Brennan, I, reflecting on the fate of my brother John, remarked to Mr. Brennan that it was hard that John should be hung upon the proof against him, when I had Nicholas' gun in my keeping all the while. Mr. Brennan immediately asked if it was true that I had the gun; and on assuring him it was, he reproved me in very severe terms for having omitted to disclose the fact long ago, and instantly went out to communicate the intelligence to a neighbor, Mr. Lewis Devlin. In a few minutes Mr. Brennan returned, accompanied by Mr. Devlin, when they questioned me particularly about the facts; and only my narrating them substantially as here given, they united in denouncing my conduct as highly culpable, but finally admitted that as it seemed I had believed myself liable to be again tried, even after my acquittal, I was not so unpardonably blamable as I at first appeared. Mr. Devlin, as I am informed, immediately acquainted his brother, John Devlin, of Pawtucket, with these facts, and in the afternoon of Thursday, he, John Devlin, called upon me, and, after hearing my statement, insisted on my going with him to Cranston, and shewing him the gun and pistol. This I did that afternoon, finding the gun where I left it, and the pistol in Nicholas' trunk. After exhibiting them to him, I replaced them—the gun under the floor, and the pistol in the trunk—and there, so far as I know, they still are. My mother, sister, and my little girl, are the occupants of the house, and they now know that the gun and pistol are in the house.

Mr. Devlin, after seeing the gun and pistol, urged me, as a matter of duty to myself, to my brother, and to the public, to make affidavit to the facts above set forth:—In accordance with his request, and in obedience to the dictates of my own conscience, this affidavit is made.

(Signed,)   WILLIAM GORDON

Providence sc.—In the city of Providence, this 10th day of February, A. D. 1845, appeared William Gordon, and made oath that the afore written affidavit by him subscribed, is true in all its parts.

Before me,   J. C. HIDDEN,
Justice of the Peace.

I, SIMON MATHEWSON, of Scituate, in the County of Providence, on oath, declare and say:

That I was one of the jurors empannelled in the case of the State vs. Nicholas S. Gordon, charged as the instigator of, and as accessory to the murder of the late Mr. Amasa Sprague, at the last September term of the Supreme Court; that after the termination of the trial of said Nicholas and the dismissal of the jury, feeling a strong desire to see the scene of the murder and the neighboring grounds, I determined to visit the ground as I returned to my home, being obliged to travel only about a mile out of my way to accomplish my purpose: that accordingly, on the day of my dismissal by the Court, in company with Mr. Lewis Chapman, a young man then in my employ, whom I found in Olneyville, I proceeded towards the said scene of the murder, taking the Johnston road: and that while on the Johnston road, and when about half a mile from Fenner's tavern, we were over-taken by a wagon, containing three men, one of whom I recognized as William Gordon, a brother of the said Nicholas, with whom I entered into conversation, which continued until we reached Dyer's Bridge.

And further I declare and say that on arriving at said bridge I requested that some one of the three would accompany me and Mr. Chapman over the grounds, to point out to us the several places and objects referred to in the trial, and that the said William Gordon complied, and with us traversed the fields from that place round to the spot of the murder, and from thence to the bridge over Hawkins' Hole, and up the driftway towards the Gordon house.

That a few minutes after crossing the bridge, I in the course of con[ver]sation expressed my opinion that John Gordon could not possibly have been guilty of the murder; but as to Nicholas, I could not speak so positively; there were some strong

circumstances against him,—such as owning the gun with which unquestionably
the deed was done, &c. &c. I noticed that when I made mention of the gun,
William seemed much affected, even shedding tears, and after a minute or two,
said in a positive tone, it was not Nicholas' gun that was used in the perpetration of
the crime and was produced in court. I then told him it had been proved to be
Nicholas's gun; for Nicholas told Dr. Cleaveland that he had a gun, which he
bought at Almy's auction; and the negro Francis had sworn that the gun in Court
was the one he left with Almy to sell. The said William deeply affected, reiterated
his denial, and when I, continuing to argue upon the evidence, asked him where
Nicholas's gun was that he bought of Almy, said he knew where it was, and would
show it to me if I would go to the house. To this I readily assented, and in company
with said William and said Chapman proceeded to the Gordon house. William
leading us immediately to the upper story and proceeding to remove a piece of
cloth carpeting from the floor, and then a piece of the flooring boards. From the
cavity thus opened he took out a gun, rather short, with a small bore, a percussion
lock, and half stocked, somewhat rusty, with iron trimmings, declaring that that
was Nicholas' gun, that he put it there on the evening of the day that Nicholas and
John were arrested, taking it from the small room below. He said also, that the
reason of his secreting the gun was that in his own country the bare possession of a
gun was a crime, and knowing that his brothers had been arrested he feared that
the finding of a gun in the house would be disadvantageous to them.

On my enquiring why he had not disclosed this fact before, he said that after he
was himself arrested on the day following, he feared to do so, lest it should
prejudice his case. The said William also said that he had never shown the gun to
any one since its secretion until this time, and it is my impression that he requested
me not to disclose the facts he had communicated. I have, however, frequently
spoken of them to my acquaintances, both on that day and since.

Signed: SIMON MATHEWSON.

Providence, sc. In the city of Providence, this eighth day of February, 1845 then
personally appeared Simon Mathewson and made oath that the facts and statements contained in the foregoing affidavit by him signed are true.

Before me,
            THOMAS A. JENCKES, Justice of the Peace

I, LEWIS CHAPMAN, of Olneyville, in the county of Providence, on oath declare
and say,

That I have listened attentively to the affidavit this day made by Mr. Simon
Mathewson, of Scituate, in which he represents me as having accompanied him in

APPENDIX

a visit to the scene of the murder of the late Mr. Amasa Sprague, and having been present at a conversation with Wm Gordon, near Hawkins' Hole, and at a conversation afterwards with the same person in the upper room of the Gordon house, when the said William produced a gun which he averred to be the gun of his brother Nicholas:—that the said affidavit has been twice read in my hearing—and that my recollection of the facts in that affidavit set forth, corresponds in every important particular with that of Mr. Mathewson, as therein stated.

(Signed,)   LEWIS CHAPMAN.

Providence sc.—In the city of Providence, this eighth day of February, 1845, there personally appeared Lewis Chapman, and made oath to the truth of the facts and statements in the foregoing affidavit by him signed.

Before me,
THOMAS A. JENCKES, Justice of the Peace.

I, Thomas Cleavland, [*sic*] of Providence, in the county of Providence, declare and say,

That a few days after the commitment of Nicholas S. Gordon to prison, charged with the murder of Mr. Amasa Sprague, he informed me that he owned a gun, and only one gun; that it was a half stocked gun, which he bought at Almy's auction room; and that it was in his store on the day of his arrest, he having seen it there, and placed it behind or near the oil can, taking it up from the floor, after a dog had thrown it down.

I further declare and say, that I believe it was the information thus given me by said Nicholas, which led to an examination of Almy's book, and to the discovery of the fact that Francis left a gun at Almy's to be sold, and to the summoning of Francis as a witness for the government.

And further I declare and say, that I was a witness on the part of the government, in the trial of Nicholas S. Gordon, and then testified to the facts set forth in the first paragraph of this affidavit.

(Signed)   THOMAS CLEAVELAND

Providence, sc. In the city of Providence this 10th day of February, A.D. 1845, appeared Thomas Cleaveland and made affirmation that the above written facts and statements by him subscribed, are true in all their parts. Before me,

J. C. Hidden, Justice of the Peace.

Appendix

State of Rhode Island
and
Providence Plantations

Executive Department
Providence Feby 10th 1845

On the petition of John Gordon, now confined in prison under sentence of death, "for a reprieve until the end of the next Session of the General Assembly", the Executives has bestowed it's [*sic*] deliberate attention and consideration.

This petition is presented to the Executive on this Tenth day of February 1845.

The petitioner was *convicted* at the March Term of the Supreme Court, 1844, and sentence was passed on him the following Term.

Four sessions of the General Assembly have been holden since *conviction*, and two sessions since sentence was passed.

The Executive has no power to *reprieve*, excepting that which is given by Section 4 of Article 7, of the Constitution, in the following words—"He shall have power to grant reprieve *after conviction*, in all cases except those of impeachment, *until the end of the next session of the General Assembly*"—thus limiting the *exercise* of the power to a *specific term*, viz;—to the time between "*conviction* and the end of the next session of the General Assembly." *Without* this provision the Executive would have no power to reprieve for *anytime*. And limited as the term is by the *provision itself*, within which the power may be *exercised*, and that term having expired, it must be readily perceived that the Executive has no *constitutional* power to grant a reprieve on this petition.

Notes

1. The Murder

1. In order to allow for narrative flow, we have summarized prosecution testimony establishing time, place, and probable motives that led to the indictment of the three Gordon brothers. Cushing's map locates the murder scene and shows the pattern of footprints leading to Nicholas Gordon's house that substantiated the village's suspicion of the Gordons' guilt.

2. The printing of calico cloth required intricate chemical and mechanical procedures. These are described in George S. White, *Memoir of Samuel Slater, The Father of American Manufactures* (Philadelphia, 1836), 395–404.

3. These rumors were exploited by the prosecution in examining witnesses and summing up evidence. Later writers were to use them to question the guilt of the brothers or the fairness of John's execution, as well as to suggest additional motives and clues that the murder investigation ignored. See Garret Byrnes, "The Sprague Murder Case," *Providence Evening Bulletin*, May 17–May 23, 1933, and Dean P. Butman, "His Murder Changed Rhode Island Law," *Rhode Island Yearbook 1968* (Providence, 1968), 108–14.

4. *Transcript*, October 16, 1844. Richard Knight, who had been taken prisoner as a spy by the Dorrites, was a prosecution witness in Dorr's treason trial, testifying as to conditions in the enemy camp at Chepachet.

5. *Providence Journal*, June 29, 1896.

6. Patrick T. Conley and Matthew J. Smith, *Catholicism in Rhode Island: The Formative Era* (Providence, 1976), 53.

7. *Providence Journal*, January 2, 1844. Although the members of the central committee were not named by the *Providence Journal*, it is known that Richard Knight, a Sprague employee, was a member, and undoubtedly a member of the Sprague family was included. Certainly, once he returned from Washington, Senator William Sprague took over control of the investigation and any information gathered by the central committee.

8. Ibid.

9. Ibid., January 3, 1844.

10. Edward [Edwin] C. Larned and William Knowles, eds., *The Trial of John Gordon and William Gordon Charged with the Murder of Amasa Sprague, Before the Supreme Court of Rhode Island, March Term, 1844*, 2d ed. (Providence: Sidney S. Rider, 1884), 86. Subsequent references to this edition will be cited in the text as *Trial*.

Because of widespread public interest in the Gordon trial, and with the agreement of the court, no accounts of the trial were published until after the verdicts were pronounced. At that time, the Providence *Transcript* rushed into print a pamphlet edition dated March 1844 that contained only the Cushing map of the murder scene, the opening arguments of the prosecution and the defense, and summaries of prosecution testimony. This edition lacked defense testimony and cross-examination and the closing arguments of both the prosecution and the defense, which were published in subsequent editions along with an eyewitness account of John Gordon's execution. These various versions carried Edwin C. Larned's name as reporter.

Published separately (but sometimes included in later versions of the *Transcript* publication and dated March 1844) was an Appendix reprinting John Gordon's petition for a reprieve to the governor in February 1845, affidavits by William Gordon, Simon Mathewson, and others supporting his request, the defense lawyer's letter to the governor, and the governor's reply. Many of these versions are to be found in the Rhode Island Historical Society Library and the John Hay Library (Brown University): *A Full Report of the Arguments of Thomas F. Carpenter, Samuel Y. Atwell, and Joseph M. Blake, Attorney General in the Case of the State vs. John and William Gordon for the Murder of Amasa Sprague* (Providence, 1844). Citations in the text to this edition will be to *Full Report*.

Rider's edition (called the second) contains the most complete account of the trial and includes the Cushing map, testimony of prosecution witnesses, a new preface that provides information on the choosing of the jury, names of jurors, defense testimony and cross-examinations, closing arguments by both the prosecution and the defense, and John Gordon's petition for a new trial. Rider does not reprint the *Full Report*'s Appendix containing the petition, affidavits of February 10, 1845, letter to the governor and his reply. Rider does add a short summary account of the efforts by John Gordon's lawyers to convince the court, the state legislature, and the governor to reconsider the verdict. Rider (1833–1917), a Providence bibliophile and bookseller, must have had access to Larned's stenographic notes of the trial. The notes are no longer among the Providence County Court records presently stored in the Providence College Library.

11. *Providence Journal*, January 3, 1844.

12. Ibid., January 8, 1844.

13. Ibid., January 3, 1844.
14. Ibid., January 8, 1844.

2. Background to Murder

1. Marvin E. Gettleman, *The Dorr Rebellion: A Study in American Radicalism, 1833–1849* (New York, 1973), 12–18.
2. In 1840 under the royal charter, 421 citizens of Providence were disqualified from voting even though they "were taxed upon personal property owned by them in the city, amounting to between one and two millions of dollars." Similarly, in 1841, 463 such nonvoters were taxed on two million dollars and in 1843, the last year of the charter, 436 "non-voters were so taxed upon the same amount" (U.S. Congress, House, 28th Cong., 1st session, Report 546, *Rhode Island—Interference of the Executive in the Affairs of,* June 7, 1844, 355).
3. Rhode Island did not abolish the real estate qualification for state and federal elections until 1888, but even then it was kept for financial town meetings and local elections.
4. "The People's Constitution, Article I, 3," Gettleman, *The Dorr Rebellion,* 206. Gettleman provides an extensive analysis of the radical roots of the Dorr Rebellion. In his brief summary of the Dorr war in *The Age of Jackson* (Boston, 1953), Arthur M. Schlesinger, Jr., overemphasizes the liberal nature of the 1843 Rhode Island Constitution, relying on the early commentary on the Dorr war by Arthur May Mowry, a conservative historian (*The Dorr War: Or, The Constitutional Struggle in Rhode Island* [Providence, 1901]).
5. Amasa and William Sprague had both originally supported the suffrage movement and the People's Constitution. William Sprague's vote to ratify Dorr's constitution is a matter of public record:

> I am an American citizen, of the age of twenty-one years and have my permanent residence or home, in this state. I am qualified to vote under the existing laws of this State.
>
> I vote for the constitution formed by the convention of the people assembled at Providence, and which was proposed to the people by said convention on the 18th day of November, 1841.
>
> WILLIAM SPRAGUE
> [This vote was given in Warwick.]

However, after William Sprague was elected U.S. senator by the Rhode Island General Assembly in February 1842, with the help of reformist Dorrites, he actively opposed the suffragists. He was listed among a group of former Dorrites

NOTES TO BACKGROUND TO MURDER

who became "among the most violent persecutors of the Suffrage party" (U.S. Congress, report 546, 354).

6. Gettleman, *The Dorr Rebellion,* 63.

7. *Providence Press,* May 7, 1881.

8. See Mowry, *The Dorr War* and Gettleman, *The Dorr Rebellion* for a detailed account of events leading up to the Dorrite defeat at Chepachet.

9. *Providence Journal,* April 8, 1844. On March 15, 1844 nearly a year after the new constitution went into effect, over seventy-five naturalized American citizens residing in Rhode Island, many of them prominent members of the Irish community, including Jeremiah Baggott, Patrick O'Connell, Henry Duff, and others, petitioned the U.S. Congress for redress of their grievance of disenfranchisement. They complained that under the new Rhode Island Constitution the great majority of them were debarred "from the most important political right, that of partaking as voters, in the choice of their representatives and other officers. . . ." They rightly pointed out that a real estate qualification is difficult for many men to meet, especially in a small and populous state (Rhode Island was the most densely populated state in the Union at the time). They also, as part of their grievance, stated that "the *negroes* of this State [have] the right of suffrage, as freely as it is accorded to any native citizen of the United States, thereby degrading us below the negro population."

10. Peter J. Coleman, *The Transformation of Rhode Island, 1790–1860* (Providence, 1963), 262. The People's Constitution would have provided for a secret ballot.

11. Ibid., 244. Like the Spragues, Allen owned calico print works and employed many Irish immigrants, but as an urban Democrat businessman he believed he could control his workers' votes by extending suffrage; the rural Spragues, allied with the conservative wing of the party, came to believe they could control votes by limiting suffrage.

12. Benjamin Knight, *History of the Sprague Families of Rhode Island: Cotton Manufacturers and Calico Printers* (Santa Cruz, Calif., 1881), 4–9. See also *Representative Men and Old Families of Rhode Island* (Chicago, 1908), 1:415–16.

13. Knight, *History of the Sprague Families,* 9.

14. Paul Goodman, *Towards a Christian Republic: Antimasonry and the Great Transition in New England, 1826–1836* (New York, 1988), 208.

15. Ibid., 206.

16. Joseph Brennan, *Social Conditions in Industrial Rhode Island, 1820–1860* (Washington, 1940), 25.

17. Joseph A. A. Coccia, "The Cranston Print Works—Its Economic Significance to the City of Cranston, and Its Influence on the Political, Social and Industrial Life of the City and the State of Rhode Island" (M.A. thesis, Rhode Island College, 1955), 35.

18. White, *Memoir of Samuel Slater,* 404.

19. Rhode Island Historical Preservation Commission, *Providence Industrial Sites* (Providence, 1981), 49.

20. Coleman, *The Transformation of Rhode Island,* 128.

21. See John Coolidge, *Mill and Mansion: A Study of Architecture and Society in Lowell, Massachusetts, 1820–1865* (1942; Amherst, Mass., 1993), 9–27, and William H. Pierson, Jr., *Technology and the Picturesque, the Corporate and the Early Gothic Styles,* vol. 2 of *American Buildings and Their Architects* (New York, 1978), 28–90.

22. *Providence Journal,* May 10, 1832.

23. Brennan, *Social Conditions in Industrial Rhode Island,* 32.

24. Coleman, *The Transformation of Rhode Island,* 234.

25. Paul Buhle, Scott Molloy, and Gail Sansbury, eds., *A History of Rhode Island Working People* (Providence, 1983), 10.

26. Brennan, *Social Conditions in Industrial Rhode Island,* 44.

27. Ibid., 50.

28. Ibid., 52.

29. Buhle, Molloy, and Sansbury, *A History of Rhode Island Working People,* 13.

30. Patrick T. Conley, *Democracy in Decline: Rhode Island's Constitutional Development, 1776–1841* (Providence, 1977), 274.

31. Rhode Island Historical Preservation Commission, *South Providence, Providence* (Providence, 1978), 13.

32. "Much of Dorr's support came from the under-represented laborers of the West Side, for it was this new class of poor and landless workers who were effectively excluded from voting by the property requirement. Entrenched social sanctions also prevented the native property owners from selling land to Irish investors, who were forced to purchase through 'dummy' owners in order to acquire property of their own and thereby qualify as voters" (Rhode Island Historical Preservation Commission, *The West Side, Providence* [Providence, 1976], 12).

33. See George Potter, *To the Golden Door: The Story of the Irish in Ireland and America* (Boston, 1960), 286–300, for a detailed account of the riot.

34. In March 1855 a near riot occurred in Providence at the Sisters of Mercy Convent near the Catholic church, sparked by a rumor that a young woman had been forced to join the convent against her will. The mob dispersed when the rumor proved to be false, but such was the atmosphere in Rhode Island at the height of the popularity of the Know-Nothing Party and its nativistic, anti-Catholic prejudices that a riotous mob could assemble on the strength of a rumor (ibid., 424).

35. Conley and Smith, *Catholicism in Rhode Island,* 114.

36. Conley, *Democracy in Decline,* 319.

37. Oscar Handlin, *Boston's Immigrants, 1790–1880: A Study in Acculturation,* rev. and enl. ed. (New York, 1970), 242. For a more recent study of the Boston Irish see Dennis P. Ryan, *Beyond the Ballot Box* (Amherst, Mass., 1983).

38. Handlin, *Boston's Immigrants,* 250–51.
39. Ryan, *Beyond the Ballot Box,* 21.
40. Handlin, *Boston's Immigrants,* 48, 51.
41. Thomas R. Hazard, *Report on the Poor and Insane in Rhode Island (1851)* (New York, 1973), 25–28, 93.
42. Potter, *To the Golden Door,* 442.
43. Conley and Smith, *Catholicism in Rhode Island,* 32–33.
44. *Boston Pilot,* October 21, 1840.
45. Cranston Town Council Minutes, Cranston Town Hall, vol. 4, April 6, 1840, 125.
46. Knight, *History of the Sprague Families,* 10.
47. U.S. Congress, report 546, 561.
48. Cranston Town Council Minutes, vol. 4, April 5, 1841, 141, Cranston Town Hall.
49. Cranston Land Evidence Records, D15, 539–40, March 26, 1842, Cranston Town Hall.
50. Only about one-third of all adult white males in Rhode Island were classified as freemen in 1841, most of them being native-born Americans.
51. Cranston Financial Town Meeting Records, vol. 3, August 30, 1842, 182, Cranston Town Hall.
52. Cranston Town Council Minutes, vol. 4, April 3, 1842, 182, Cranston Town Hall.
53. Advertisement in *Boston Pilot,* April 22, 1843.

3. The Prosecution

1. Potter, *To the Golden Door,* 443.
2. The supreme court of Rhode Island was made up of three members appointed by the legislature in 1835: Hon. Job Durfee (chief justice), Hon. Levi Haile (associate justice), and Hon. William R. Staples (associate justice). At the June 1843 session of the legislature a law was enacted that the court was to consist of a chief justice and three associate justices. In 1843 Hon. George A. Brayton joined the court as an associate justice; he succeeded Durfee as chief justice in 1847. All four judges presided at the three Gordon trials as well as at Dorr's treason trial. All four were graduates of Brown University, as were William Potter (prosecution team), Thomas Carpenter, Samuel Y. Atwell, Samuel Currey, and John P. Knowles (defense team).
3. Gettleman, *The Dorr Rebellion,* 152–53. Conley and Smith discuss Carpenter's later conversion to Catholicism (*Catholicism in Rhode Island,* 53–54).
4. Philip English Mackey, "'The Result May Be Glorious'—Anti-Gallows Move-

ment in Rhode Island, 1838–1852," *Rhode Island History* 33.1 (1974): 20. Staples and Atwell were members of the committee appointed by the legislature to revise the state's penal code. At that time, Atwell was a member from Glocester. For a fuller discussion of Atwell's career and legal philosophy, see Abraham Payne, *Reminiscences of the Rhode Island Bar* (Providence, 1885), 97–102. Atwell was ill during the final arguments presented by the defense in John and William Gordon's trial.

5. Gettleman, *The Dorr Rebellion*, 64. Payne, *Reminiscences*, 29.

6. *Biographical Cyclopedia of Representative Men of Rhode Island* (Providence, 1881), 339–40.

7. For a discussion of the defense in the Avery-Cornell trial, see David Richard Kasserman, *Fall River Outrage: Life, Murder, and Justice in Early Industrial New England* (Philadelphia, 1986), 99–117, 159–85. The prosecution team at the preliminary hearing was headed by William Staples, because the attorney general was out of the state at the time of the hearing.

8. In 1833, William Staples had been appointed prosecuting attorney to assist the attorney general, then Albert C. Greene, prepare and present the state's evidence against Avery at the preliminary hearing and at the trial itself. Before the trial began, the attorney general "was joined by Dutee J. Pearce, the former attorney general of Rhode Island, who left his seat in Congress to help prosecute the case." At the very last moment, on the day when the opening argument was to be presented, Staples withdrew from the case, to the acute embarrassment of Attorney General Greene: "Staples' sudden defection was probably caused by a squabble of seniority with Dutee Pearce who, as a former attorney general and current member of Congress, may well have seen political hay in the making" (Kasserman, *Fall River Outrage*, 131, 137). Greene may have declined to take part in the Gordon trial because the same William Staples was one of the justices presiding over the trial. The incident had done Staples's career no harm.

9. *Representative Men and Old Families of Rhode Island* (Chicago, 1908), 1:55–56.

10. Gettleman, *The Dorr Rebellion*, 153.

11. *Biographical Cyclopedia of Representative Men*, 339.

12. Ibid., 390–91.

13. Charles Carroll, *Rhode Island: Three Centuries of Democracy* (New York, 1932), 3:756 n., cites State vs. Nelson 18 RI 647.

14. Kasserman, *Fall River Outrage*, 132.

15. Carroll, *Rhode Island*, 3:760.

16. The fact that the attorney general did not ask Susan Field to identify the gun and the pistol found near the scene of the crime as belonging to Nicholas Gordon might suggest that she would be unable to connect Gordon with the evidence. But the prosecution did not need her testimony on this point, since others had connected the murder weapon with the Gordons. The defense counsel did not

follow through in cross-examination for good reason. Susan Field was a hostile witness. Sensing a trap laid by the prosecution, Atwell could ill afford the possibility she would positively identify the gun as belonging to Nicholas. It is one thing to attack a witness's direct testimony during cross-examination in order to attempt to make the witness contradict it or at least weaken its impact. It is quite another to give a witness an opportunity to make further damaging statements. The wise and prudent course would be to attack Susan Field's character, which is what the defense counsel did.

17. Cranston Town Council Minutes, vol. 4, July 29, 1843, 194, Cranston Town Hall.

4. The Defense

1. Payne, *Reminiscences*, 5.
2. *Cyclopedia of Representative Men*, 258.
3. Payne, *Reminiscences*, 90.
4. *Cyclopedia of Representative Men*, 35.
5. *Providence Journal*, January 3, 1844.
6. If Amasa Sprague was a temperance advocate, his advocacy was highly selective, for the only liquor license he opposed that summer was Nicholas Gordon's.
7. Larned not only testified in this trial about his notes taken at the hearing before the examining magistrate in the prison, but he was also called to testify in Nicholas's trial about the notes he had taken of Walter Beattie's testimony before the magistrate (*Transcript*, October 19, 1844).
8. *Providence Journal*, January 3, 1844.
9. Hugh Brody, *Inishkillane: Change and Decline in the West of Ireland* (New York, 1974), 109.
10. Conley and Smith, *Catholicism in Rhode Island*, 128.
11. Jeremiah Baggott was an agent for the weekly in Providence, collecting money for subscriptions. It is known that Nicholas Gordon picked up the paper at Baggott's shop on Sundays after mass.
12. *Transcript*, April 19, 1844.
13. *Boston Pilot*, April 27, 1844.

5. Nicholas Gordon's First Trial

1. Carroll, *Rhode Island*, 3:759.
2. *Transcript*, May 2, 1844.
3. Ibid., May 3, 1844.

4. Mowry, *The Dorr War,* 243. Algerine was a pejorative term used to designate a member of the Law and Order Party.

Two of the three jurors were dismissed as already having formed and expressed opinions as to Dorr's guilt or innocence, and the third was impeached as being disqualified on the same grounds (Frances H. Whipple McDougall, *Might and Right by a Rhode Islander* [Providence, 1844], 319).

5. Cited in McDougall, *Might and Right,* 318 (italics in the original).

6. Mowry, *The Dorr War,* 245.

7. Gettleman, *The Dorr Rebellion,* 11.

8. Mowry, *The Dorr War,* 245.

9. Ibid., 228. Two Cranston farmers, Andrew Essex and Charles A. Slocum, had also been arrested for having accepted the office of justice of the peace and acting as moderator of a town meeting respectively. Essex faced imprisonment for one year and a fine of $2,000; Slocum, imprisonment for six months and a fine of not more than $1,000 or less than $500 (U.S. Congress, House, report 546, 71).

10. Mowry, *The Dorr War,* 235.

11. McDougall, *Might and Right,* 322.

12. Ibid.

13. Mowry, *The Dorr War,* 248.

14. Ibid., 253–54.

15. McDougall, *Might and Right,* 333–36.

16. *Boston Pilot,* July 13, 1844.

17. Brennan, *Social Conditions in Industrial Rhode Island,* 154–55.

18. Gettleman, *The Dorr Rebellion,* 167.

19. *Transcript,* October 10, 1844.

20. Payne, *Reminiscences,* 90–96. Samuel Currey, a naturalized citizen, was born in New Brunswick, Canada, graduated from Brown University, studied law in the office of Albert C. Greene, and was an anti-Dorrite during the Dorr Rebellion, serving in a military company. He later served as counsel for the Hartford, Providence and Fishkill Railroad, an enterprise supported by William Sprague, who was a major stockholder.

21. *The Historical Catalogue of Brown University, 1764–1934* (Providence, 1936), 161. Hart was a member of the class of 1841.

22. *Transcript,* October 15, 1844. The two trials of Nicholas Gordon were covered by the daily newspapers, although testimony deemed repetitious or part of the earlier trial was left out. As with the first trial, the transcripts of these trials were also reprinted in small editions by the *Transcript.* None of these accounts seems to have survived.

23. Ibid., October 22, 1844.

24. Ibid.

25. Ibid., October 26, 1844.

26. Ibid.

27. Mowry, *The Dorr War,* 324. In 1854, the state legislature attempted to overthrow the verdict of the supreme court in the Dorr case. The court's rejection of this attempt at legislative control of the judiciary reinforced the court's independence, ironically one of the goals of the Dorr Constitution.

28. *Transcript,* October 15, 1844.

29. Ibid., October 16, 1844.

30. Ibid.

31. Ibid. Italics added.

32. Ibid.

33. Cranston Town Council Minutes, vol. 4, June 24, 1843, 192, Cranston Town Hall.

34. Ibid., March 25, 1843, 178–79.

35. Ibid., April 3, 1843, 181. The General Assembly in 1841 had passed a law enabling the town councils of Rhode Island to grant licenses for retailing strong liquors. Brennan is mistaken in stating that the Rhode Island General Assembly had passed a statewide prohibition law in effect from 1841 to 1845 (Brennan, *Social Conditions in Industrial Rhode Island,* 85–86). Local option was then in effect. It was not until 1852 that a statewide prohibition law was passed, based on the Maine law. This was repealed in 1863. William Potter's brother Elisha led the repeal movement.

36. Cranston Town Council Minutes, vol. 4, July 29, 1843, 194, Cranston Town Hall.

37. *Transcript,* October 16, 1844.

38. Ibid.

39. Ibid.

40. Ibid., October 18, 1844.

41. Ibid.

42. Ibid.

43. Ibid.

44. Ibid.

45. Ibid.

46. Ibid.

47. Ibid.

48. Ibid., October 19, 1844.

49. Ibid.

50. Ibid.

51. Cranston Town Council Minutes, vol. 4, November 2, 1844, 267, Cranston Town Hall.

52. *Transcript,* October 19, 1844.

53. Ibid.

54. Ibid.
55. Ibid.
56. *Transcript,* October 22, 1844.
57. Ibid.
58. Ibid.
59. Ibid.

6. The Execution of John Gordon

1. See our Appendix, for the complete text of the affidavits of William Gordon, Simon Mathewson, and Lewis Chapman describing their actions. They appeared in Larned's Appendix to the *Full Report* along with Knowles's letter to the governor and Governor Fenner's reply.

2. Although William had visited his mother about four o'clock in the afternoon on the day of the murder, he would have had to return to his room in Providence by six o'clock or thereabouts if, as he claimed in the affidavit, he knew nothing about the murder until the next day. The murder was general knowledge in Cranston by seven o'clock at the latest.

3. Carroll, *Rhode Island,* 3:761.

4. Byrnes, "The Sprague Murder Case," May 22, 1933, 10.

5. *Transcript,* January 14, 1845.

6. Ibid.

7. Ibid., January 17, 1845. There was, however, a condition to the amnesty (which had been petitioned by his parents). He would have to swear an oath of allegiance to the present Rhode Island government and constitution—a condition the anti-Dorrites knew Dorr would refuse, since earlier he had refused such an offer. The pro-Dorr forces, led by Fenner Brown, opposed the bill unless they knew Dorr would accept the attached condition. The vote was 49 for, 13 against.

8. Ibid., January 18, 1845.

9. See our Appendix for the text of John Knowles's covering letter and Governor Fenner's reply.

10. *Transcript,* February 14, 1845.

11. *Boston Pilot,* February 22, 1845.

12. Mackey, "'The Result May Be Glorious,'" 19.

13. *Transcript,* February 14, 1845.

14. Charles Hoffmann and Tess Hoffmann, *North by South: The Two Lives of Richard James Arnold* (Athens, Ga., 1988), 88.

15. Louis P. Masur, *Rites of Execution: Capital Punishment and the Transformation of American Culture, 1776–1865* (New York, 1989), 5.

16. Hoffmann and Hoffmann, *North by South,* 89–90.

17. Brennan, *Social Conditions in Industrial Rhode Island,* 149–50.

18. *Transcript,* February 15, 1845. Sullivan Dorr, Thomas Dorr's father, was one of the eyewitnesses, standing so close to John Gordon that he could almost "reach out and touch him." He was present not as the father of Thomas Dorr but as a prominent citizen, a merchant-industrialist, representing the community at large.

19. Masur, *Rites of Execution,* 111.

20. *Transcript,* February 14, 1845.

21. Ibid.

22. Ibid., February 15, 1845.

23. Conley and Smith, *Catholicism in Rhode Island,* 55 (italics added).

24. *Transcript,* February 14, 1845.

25. Ibid., February 24, 1845. The editor of the *Transcript* wrote at some length to refute the *New World Weekly* because even he had to admit it was a responsible journal of wide circulation and not a rag.

26. Ibid., February 14, 1845.

27. Ibid.

28. Ibid., February 15, 1845.

29. *Providence Journal,* January 5, 1900, reprints an eyewitness account (source unknown) of John Gordon's funeral procession.

7. Nicholas Gordon's Second Trial

1. Gettleman, *The Dorr Rebellion,* 172.

2. Mackey, "The Result May Be Glorious," 23. Mackey does not think, however, that John Gordon's execution had any direct effect on the abolition of the death penalty in 1852 (28).

3. *Transcript,* April 8, 1845.

4. Richard M. Bayles, *The History of Providence County, Rhode Island* (New York, 1891), 2:621–22. Isaac Saunders was engaged in cotton manufacturing and was at various times a member of the Rhode Island General Assembly, president of the Scituate Town Council, justice of the peace, and president of the Citizens Union Bank. Like Hidden, the foreman at the trial of John and William Gordon, he was a solid citizen with impeccable conservative credentials.

5. *Transcript,* April 10, 1845.

6. Ibid. (italics in original text).

7. Ibid., April 18, 1844 (italics added).

8. Ibid., April 11, 1845.

9. Ibid., April 10, 1845.

10. Ibid., April 12, 1845. Tately's name is spelled Tatiby in the *Transcript* and Tately in William Gordon's affidavit.

11. Ibid.

12. Ibid.

13. Ibid.

14. Ibid., April 14, 1845.

15. Ibid.

16. Ibid., April 11, 1845.

17. Ibid., April 12, 1845 (italics added).

18. Ibid., April 16, 1845.

19. Ibid., April 12, 1845.

20. Ibid., April 14, 1845.

21. Ibid. Fifteen years later William Sprague's nephew, Amasa's son William, was reported to have spent $125,000 to buy fraudulent Irish votes in order to win the race for governor of Rhode Island. A poem appeared in a handbill at the time extolling the wit and wisdom of one Paddy McFlynn:

> So says he, 'Mister Sprague, it's myself that would vote,
> But, be Jabers, I've nayther a shirt nor a coat;
> And me trousers is missin, and faith 'twould be quare,
> If I'd be after voting with nothing to wear.'
>
> . . . .
>
> And somehow he got him a coat and a hat
> With brogans and calico shirt and all that,
> 'But,' says Pat, 'it's a demicrat nonetheless,
> In dacent, conservative calico dress.'

Cited in Robert A. Wheeler, "Fifth Ward Irish—Immigrant Mobility in Providence, 1850–1870," *Rhode Island History* 32.2 (1973):55. Wheeler mistakenly identifies the election as being for the U.S. Senate.

22. *Transcript,* April 14, 1845.

23. Ibid., April 15, 1845.

24. Ibid.

25. Ibid.

26. Ibid., April 16, 1845.

27. Ibid.

28. Ibid., April 18, 1845.

29. Ibid.

30. Ibid. The spelling of the Irish names is obviously approximate.

31. Probate Records of the Municipal Court of the City of Providence, Estate of Nicholas S. Gordon, "Inventory," Book 7, January 18, 1847, 284, and "Report of the Commissioners," Book 2, March 8, 1848, 361, Providence City Hall.

32. Mackey, "'The Result May Be Glorious,'" 19–30.

33. *Providence Journal,* October 15, 1878.

34. Town of Cranston Land Evidence Records, D18, 314, Cranston Town Hall.

35. Ibid., D24, 257.

8. Who Killed Amasa Sprague?

1. Knight, *History of the Sprague Families,* 29.

2. Coccia, "The Cranston Print Works," 24–25.

3. Wilfred H. Munro, *Picturesque Rhode Island* (Providence, 1881), 175.

4. *Transcript,* October 18, 1844.

5. Ibid., April 16, 1845.

6. Knight, *History of the Sprague Families,* 30–31.

7. Ibid., 31–32.

8. Carroll, *Rhode Island,* 3:764.

9. Mathias P. Harpin, *The High Road to Zion* (Centreville, R.I., 1976), 146.

10. Carroll, *Rhode Island,* 3:764 provides a fitting epilogue to the rise and fall of the Sprague empire:

> The Sprague factories in Rhode Island, Connecticut and Maine in 1873 provided employment for 10,000 to 12,000 operatives at 280,000 spindles and twenty-eight printing machines, the output of which exceeded 1,000,000 pieces of cloth annually. The Spragues were enterprising, and members of the family had invented and introduced improvements on calico printing presses, and in dyeing and printing processes. Their iron factories made and marketed the Sprague mowing machine, horseshoes made by a new process, as well as nails of new design. They owned and operated the street railway in Providence, as well as a line of freight and passenger steamers between Providence and Fishkill, the line of which had been constructed to pass through one of their factory villages [Spraguesville]. They were interested by investment and stockholding in a great variety of manufacturing and other corporations. They owned real estate in almost every town in Rhode Island, additional to factories, factory sites, water rights and factory villages. In Maine, besides a factory operating 34,000 spindles and a water right at Augusta on the Kennebec River, they held land as sites for other factories, and vast areas of timber lands with sawmills as part of a project for a lumber company. Westward their holdings of land extended to Kansas and Texas; their purchase of a water right and land at Columbia, South Carolina, suggests that they had grasped the possibility of manufac-

turing cotton cloth in the South as supply for their vast converting factories in Rhode Island and Connecticut. The conception of expansion was gigantic, and the Spragues through years of uninterrupted success had become convinced of their own invincibility. The house had risen because of the tremendous ability of the family for several generations.

Bibliography

"Affidavit of William Gordon, Simon Mathewson, Lewis Chapman, Petition of John Gordon, etc." February 10, 1845. Providence. In *A Full Report of the Arguments of Thomas F. Carpenter,* . . . see Larned, Edwin C.

Amnesty International U.S.A. *The Death Penalty: Developments in 1987.* New York, 1988.

Angell, Joseph K., ed. *Reports of Cases Argued and Determined in the Supreme Court of Rhode Island,* 1:179–93. Boston, 1847.

Arnold, Noah J. "The Valley of the Pawtuxet." *The Narragansett Historical Register* 6 (1888): 222–59.

Bagnall, William R. *Textile Industries of the United States.* Vol. 1. Cambridge, Mass., 1893.

Bayles, Richard M. *The History of Providence County, Rhode Island.* New York, 1891.

Bedau, Hugo Adam, ed. *The Death Penalty in America.* 3rd ed. New York, 1982.

Biographical Cyclopedia of Representative Men of Rhode Island. Providence, 1881.

Brennan, Joseph. *Social Conditions in Industrial Rhode Island, 1820–1860.* Washington, 1940.

Brody, Hugh. *Inishkillane: Change and Decline in the West of Ireland.* New York, 1974.

Buhle, Paul, Scott Molloy, and Gail Sansbury, eds. *A History of Rhode Island Working People.* Providence, 1983.

Butman, Dean P. "His Murder Changed Rhode Island Law." *Rhode Island Yearbook, 1968,* 108–14. Providence, 1968.

Byrnes, Garret. "The Sprague Murder Case." In 6 parts. *Providence Evening Bulletin,* May 17–23, 1933.

Carroll, Charles. *Rhode Island: Three Centuries of Democracy.* New York, 1932.

Chase, David. *An Historical Survey of Rhode Island Textile Mills.* Providence, 1969.

Ciaburri, Robert L. "The Dorr Rebellion in Rhode Island: Moderate Phase." *Rhode Island History* 26.3 (1967): 73–87.

Coccia, Joseph A. A. "The Cranston Print Works—Its Economic Significance to the City of Cranston and Its Influence on the Political, Social, and Industrial

BIBLIOGRAPHY

Life of the City and State of Rhode Island." M.A. thesis, Rhode Island College, 1955.

Coleman, Peter J. *The Transformation of Rhode Island, 1790–1860.* Providence, 1963.

Conley, Patrick T. *Democracy in Decline: Rhode Island's Constitutional Development, 1776–1841.* Providence, 1977.

———. *The Dorr Rebellion: Rhode Island's Crisis in Constitutional Government.* Providence, 1976.

Conley, Patrick T., and Matthew J. Smith. "The Case of John Gordon . . . Death Knell for the Death Penalty." *The Providence Visitor,* July 6, 1973.

———. *Catholicism in Rhode Island: The Formative Era.* Providence, 1976.

Coolidge, John. *Mill and Mansion: A Study of Architecture and Society in Lowell, Massachusetts, 1820–1865.* 2nd ed. Amherst, Mass., 1993.

Dunwell, Steve. *The Run of the Mill.* Boston, 1978.

E. W. D. "John Gordon's Grave." *Providence Sunday Journal,* January 7, 1900.

Gersuny, Carl. "Seth Luther—The Road from Chepachet." *Rhode Island History* 33.2 (1974): 47–55.

Gettleman, Marvin E. *The Dorr Rebellion: A Study in American Radicalism, 1833–1849.* New York, 1973.

Goodman, Paul. *Towards a Christian Republic: Antimasonry and the Great Transition in New England, 1826–1836.* New York, 1988.

Handlin, Oscar. *Boston's Immigrants, 1790–1880: A Study in Acculturation.* Revised and enlarged ed. New York, 1970.

Harpin, Mathias P. *The High Road to Zion.* Centreville, R.I., 1976.

Hazard, Thomas R. *Report on the Poor and Insane in Rhode Island (1851).* Reprint ed. New York, 1973.

The Historical Catalogue of Brown University, 1764–1934. Providence, 1936.

Hoffmann, Charles, and Tess Hoffmann. *North by South: The Two Lives of Richard James Arnold.* Athens, Ga., 1988.

Hook, Donald D., and Lothar Kahn. *Death in the Balance: The Debate over Capital Punishment.* Lexington, Mass., 1989.

Kasserman, David Richard. *Fall River Outrage: Life, Murder, and Justice In Early Industrial New England.* Philadelphia, 1986.

King, Dan. *The Life and Times of Thomas Wilson Dorr, with Outlines of the Political History of Rhode Island.* Boston, 1859.

Knight, Benjamin. *History of the Sprague Families of Rhode Island: Cotton Manufacturers and Calico Printers.* Santa Cruz, Calif., 1881.

Knights, Peter R. *The Plain People of Boston, 1830–1860: A Study in City Growth.* New York, 1971.

Knobel, Dale T. *Paddy and the Republic: Ethnicity and Nationality in Antebellum America.* Middletown, Conn., 1986.

Bibliography

Larned, Edwin C., reporter. A *Full Report of the Arguments of Thomas F. Carpenter, Samuel Y. Atwell and Joseph M. Blake Attorney General in the Case of the State vs. John and William Gordon for the Murder of Amasa Sprague*. Providence, 1844. In some editions appendix includes "Execution of John Gordon"; "Affidavit of William Gordon, et al."; "Petition of John Gordon"; "Letter of John P. Knowles"; and "Governor Fenner's Reply," February 1845.

Larned, Edward [Edwin] C., and William Knowles, reporters. *The Trial of John Gordon and William Gordon Charged with the Murder of Amasa Sprague, Before the Supreme Court of Rhode Island, March Term, 1844.* Providence, Sidney S. Rider, 1884.

Lemons, Stanley, and Michael A. McKenna. "Re-enfranchisement of Rhode Island Negroes." *Rhode Island History* 30.1 (1971): 3–13.

Mackey, Philip English. "'The Result May Be Glorious'—Anti-Gallows Movement in Rhode Island, 1838–1852." *Rhode Island History* 33.1 (1974): 19–31.

Magrath, C. Peter. "Optimistic Democrat: Thomas W. Dorr and the Case of Luther vs. Borden." *Rhode Island History* 29.3 and 4 (1970): 94–112.

Masur, Louis P. *Rites of Execution: Capital Punishment and the Transformation of American Culture, 1776–1865.* New York, 1989.

Mayer, Kurt B. *Economic Development and Population Growth in Rhode Island.* Providence, 1953.

Mayer, Kurt B., and Sidney Goldstein. *Migration and Economic Development in Rhode Island.* Providence, 1958.

McCarthy, Joseph. *Rhode Island Mills and Mill Villages.* Providence, 1940.

McDougall, Frances H. Whipple. *Might and Right by a Rhode Islander.* Providence, 1844.

Mowry, Arthur May. *The Dorr War or the Constitutional Struggle in Rhode Island.* Reprint ed. New York, 1970.

Munro, Wilfred H. *Picturesque Rhode Island.* Providence, 1881.

Payne, Abraham. *Reminiscences of the Rhode Island Bar.* Providence, 1885.

Pierson, William H., Jr. *Technology and the Picturesque, the Corporate and the Early Gothic Styles.* Vol. 2 of *American Buildings and Their Architects.* New York, 1978.

Potter, George. *To the Golden Door: The Story of the Irish in Ireland and America.* Boston, 1960.

Renshaw, Clifford M. *A Walking Tour of the Cranston Print Works Village.* Providence, n.d.

Representative Men and Old Families of Rhode Island. Chicago, 1908.

Rhode Island Historical Preservation Commission. *Providence Industrial Sites.* Providence, 1981.

———. *South Providence, Providence.* Providence, 1978.

———. *The West Side, Providence.* Providence, 1976.

BIBLIOGRAPHY

Ryan, Dennis P. *Beyond the Ballot Box: A Social History of the Boston Irish, 1845–1917.* Amherst, Mass., 1983.

Schlesinger, Arthur, Jr. *The Age of Jackson.* Boston, 1953.

Siracusa, Carl. *A Mechanical People: Perception of the Industrial Order of Massachusetts, 1815–1880.* Middletown, Conn., 1979.

U.S. Congress. House. *Rhode Island—Interference in the Affairs of.* 28th Cong, 1st sess. Report #546. June 7, 1844.

Wheeler, Robert A. "Fifth Ward Irish—Immigrant Mobility in Providence, 1850–1870." *Rhode Island History* 32.2 (1973): 53–61.

White, George S. *Memoir of Samuel Slater, The Father of American Manufactures.* Philadelphia, 1836.

Who Killed Amasa Sprague? The Old Stone Bank. Providence, 1932.

Wiecek, William M. "Popular Sovereignty in the Dorr War—Conservative Counterblast." *Rhode Island History* 32.2 (1973): 35–51.

Wiley, A. J. "Buried in Pawtucket." *Providence Sunday Journal,* January 7, 1900.

Wyss, Bob. " 'They Did Not Know What They Were Doing.' " *Providence Sunday Journal Magazine,* July 19, 1981, 24–26.

Index

INDEX

Bowen, Henry L., 8–9, 10–11
Bowen, Dr. Israel, xiii, 2, 3, 4
Brady, Father John, 112–14
Brennan, Patrick, 108, 153
Briggs, Andrew, 126
Burges, Walter S., 78, 125
Burrill, George R. (Senator), 78

capital punishment, xiv, xvii, 32, 107, 110–12, 115, 132, 135
Carpenter, Jeremiah, 27, 28
Carpenter, Susannah Sprague Mathewson (sister of Amasa), 17, 27
Carpenter, Thomas F., 31, 32, 33, 34, 35, 41, 47, 48, 58–61, 82, 103–4, 125, 142, 151–52, 164 n.2
Carroll, Charles, 35
Chafee, Daniel, 85, 101
Chapman, Lewis, 99–100, 151, 152–53, 154, 155–56
child labor, 20–21
Cleaveland, Dr. Thomas, 11, 85–86, 100, 150, 152, 155, 156
Coil, Edward, 3
Cole, John, 52–53
Cole, Joseph, 50–53, 68–69, 70, 103–4
Coleman, Peter J., 16
Conley, Patrick, 7–8
constitutional reform, xii, xv, 14–15, 15–16, 33, 34, 79, 109, 162 n.9
Corry, Father John, 26, 27
Costello, Michael, xiii, 1–2
Cozzens, Benjamin, 19, 96
Cranston, Robert B. (Representative), 107
Cranston, 22, 26, 27–28, 47, 90, 92, 102, 115, 119, 131–32, 133, 137, 148, 153
Cranston Print Works, xvi, 1, 2 (map),

3, 18, 19, 20, 21, 24–25, 26, 39, 52–53, 137, 144, 145
Cranston Town Council, xi, xv, xvi, 8, 25, 27–28, 87–89, 91, 93, 94, 119
Cranston Town Meeting, 27, 89
Currey, Samuel, 11, 32, 47, 67, 82, 83–84, 97, 103–4, 117, 121, 123, 151–52, 164 n.2, 167 n.20
Cushing, S. B. (surveyor), 2 (map), 23, 159 n.1

DeFoster, John, 141
DeMerritt, John, 120, 128
Democratic Party (Rhode Island), 6, 13, 14–15, 16, 18, 27, 32, 78, 117, 162 n.11
Devlin, John, 108, 151, 153–54
Devlin, Lewis, 108, 130, 153
Dexter Asylum Poor House, 26
Dorr, Thomas Wilson: Chepachet xv, 15, 86; death, xvii; defense at trial, 79–80; Dorr family history, 13; flees in exile, xii, xv; indicted for treason, xv, 12, 24; pardon, xvii, 12, 117, 129–30; proposed amnesty, 169 n.7; trial in Newport, xvi, 76–81; sentenced to life imprisonment, xvi, 81
Dorr, Sullivan, 13, 22, 31, 115, 170 n.18
Dorr Rebellion, xii, xv, 6, 13–16, 21–22, 34–35, 80, 167 n.20
Downey, William, 121, 149
Drybrook mill (Johnston), 25, 56, 125
Duff, Henry, 26, 162 n.9
Durfee, Job (Chief Justice), 14, 22, 31, 35, 39, 42, 45–46, 58–59, 60–61, 69–72, 77–78, 80, 81, 83–84, 97, 126, 130, 164 n.2
Dyer, Rodney, 57–58
Dyer's bridge, 57–58, 62, 95–96, 152, 154

INDEX

Irish immigrants, xii, 20–24, 25–26, 28, 65–66, 71, 88–89, 118, 131, 162 n.11, 171 n.21
Irish Poor Law (1838), 24

Jackson, Charles (Governor), 117, 129
James, Giles, 91–92, 121–22, 123–24
Jenckes, Thomas A., 155, 156

King, Edward, 94–95
Kingston, John, 5
Kingston, Thompson, 5, 48–49
Kingston, William, 5
Kit, Ben (Benjamin Waterman), 39, 59, 62, 72, 90, 125–26, 143
Knight, Nehemiah R., 133
Knight, Richard, 6, 18, 41, 50–51, 52, 53, 55, 58, 62, 68, 70, 87, 89, 90, 103–4, 120, 159 nn.4, 7
Knight, Sheldon, 8, 25, 101
Knight, B. B. & R., Co., 146
Knightsville (Rhode Island), 26, 133
Knowles, John P., 11, 32, 47–48, 75, 82, 102–3, 108–10, 126–27, 147, 164 n.2
Know-Nothing Party, 163 n.34

Landholder's Constitution, 15, 33, 162 n.9
Landlord and Tenant Law (Ireland), 66
Larned, Edwin C., 56–57, 60, 160 n.10, 166 n.7
Law and Order Party, 15, 16, 32, 82, 105, 117
Lawton, David, xiii, 37–38, 63
Liberation Party, 117, 129
Luther, Gardner, 38, 65
Luther, Martin, 79
Luther vs. Borden, 79

Manchester, Thadeus, 91
Masur, Louis P., 111–12
Mathewson, Obadiah, 17
Mathewson, Rollin, 58, 62, 63–64, 142
Mathewson, Simon, xvi, 99–100, 102, 103, 104, 108–9, 147, 151, 152–53, 154–56
Mathewson, Stephen, 4
M'Clocklin, Francis (McLaughlin), 57, 62, 95, 142
McCoy, Margaret, 133
Miller, Dr. Lewis L., 5, 85
Mowry, Arthur May, 79, 161 n.4

New England Workingmen's Association, 20–21
New York Herald, 10
New World Weekly, 113–14
North Burial Ground, xvi, 115

O'Brien, Dennis, 48–49
O'Brien, John, 54, 57–58, 62, 128
O'Brien, Michael, 9, 10–11, 48–50, 53, 68–69, 70, 92, 94–95
O'Brien's tailor shop (Providence), 100–101, 148–49
O'Connell, Patrick, 26, 162 n.9

Pearce, Dutee J., 165 n.8
People's Constitution (Dorr), 14–15, 24, 27, 69, 79, 84, 109, 161 n.5, 168 n.27
Pitman, Joseph S. (editor of *Transcript*), 113–14
politics of prejudice, xi, xii, xiv, 24, 118, 127, 129–30, 135–36
popular sovereignty, xii, 15–16, 32, 79–80
Portsmouth Poor House (Rhode Island), 26
Potter, Annie (Amasa's mother), 16